ANOINTING OVER PERFECTION

The Power of Perseverance in the Pursuit of Purpose!

MIKELLA HANSLEY

Anointing Over Perfection

Covered By Three Series
VOLUME 1

Anointing Over Perfection:
The Power of Perseverance in the Pursuit of Purpose!

*"Your imperfections and perseverance are your best characteristics
because they shape you for your anointing."*
-Mikella Hansley-

Contents

To my Big Awesome God and Heavenly Father — xi

Dedication to My Parents — xiii

To My Grandmother Pearlie Mae — xv

To My God Grandmother Sandra — xvii

To Pastor & First Lady Handsom — xix

To My Hometown Swainsboro — xxi

To Pastor Marcus Gill — xxiii

To My Grandmother Dora — xxv

Foreword — xxix
by Marcus Gill

Introduction — xxxi

About the Book — xxxvii

Part I

The Vision

Covered By Three: The Vision — 3

The Covered By Three Vision — 5

The Reasoning Behind Covered By Three — 7

Reasoning Behind Logo Design — 9
(I want you to notice there are three sections to my logo design)

The Triple Anointing — 11

Part II

Truth

Can You Imagine?! — 17

Unspoken — 21
The Untold Truth of My Life

Part III

The Guide

The Declaration — 43

Introduction — 45

Introduction   47

Day 1   49
Always Make Time for God

Day 2   53
Be Humble

Day 3   57
Patience

Day 4   61
Run to God

Day 5   65
Focus

Day 6   69
Be Productive

Day 7   75
Put In The Work

Day 8   79
Acceptance

Day 9   83
Peer Pressure or Just Pressure?

Day 10   87
Bad Company Corrupts Good Manners

Day 11   91
Fear

Day 12   95
Die to Self

Day 13   99
Prayer

Day 14   103
Worship and Favor

Day 15   107
Persevering in the Test

Day 16   111
Love and Forgive Your Enemies

Day 17   117
What are You Feeding Your Spirit?

Day 18   125
Don't Limit God

Day 19   131
God's Working It for Your Good

Day 20   135
Purpose

A Sneak Peek (Book Two)   141

Part IV

Other

Fighting for My Life: A Test of Faith and   145
Spiritual Warfare
A More Detailed Version of the Spiritual Warfare in Unspoken

When It All Falls Apart Seek God and It Will All   155
Make Sense: God is Drawing You to Him
Because He Wants to Show You What is in You!

We Are in the Pre-Tribulation   159

About the Author   161
Let's Connect!   167

"The journey is not about perfection,
but making *progress* through the *process*!"
-Mikella Hansley-

To my Big Awesome God and
Heavenly Father

Thank You! If I had a thousand tongues that would not be enough! Thank You for the vision and desire to write a book. I thank You for the wisdom and strength You gave me to write it. Thank You for Your reckless love and pursuing me in my mess, even when I was undeserving.

Dedication to My Parents

People would always tell me I was blessed to have two Godly parents. Honestly, for a long time, I couldn't see it. Like I knew I was blessed, but I didn't really understand just how much. All I could see is that they were being hard on me for not letting me do what other young people my age did. Now that I am older, I am so thankful for their parenting. I look over my life and everything I've accomplished, and it's because of their sacrifices, them constantly pushing me for greater, and not allowing me to do what everyone else did. I'm so grateful to have parents who listen to me, go above and beyond for me, and support my vision and goals. I have never lacked anything and had most of my wants. I am glad that I'm not like everyone else. I am me, and I am loving the woman that God is turning me into daily. I am truly grateful for my parents. I could not have asked for a better pair! Thank you so much, God! If you have two parents that are trying to keep you on the right path, you should appreciate that. Parents always know what's best! I love the story of Esther from the Bible so much because she was an only child with two Godly parents. I can relate to her a lot. When you look at me, you see the grace of God and excellent parents!

To My Grandmother
Pearlie Mae

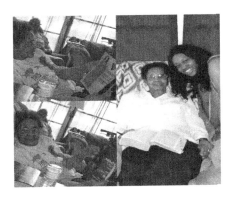

You are the best grandmother that anyone can ask for. You have created a big beautiful family. At the age of 96, you are the epitome of class, beauty, and grace. Thank you for your hard work and dedication to the family. I love how you read your Bible every day and I'm so happy that I was in a magazine with your favorite celebrity (Steve Harvey). Grandma I also love how you do your dance just because you are so happy to see me. Thank you for always loving me unconditionally and spoiling me. Thank you for the Pearlie Mae booty (My family will know what that means, haha). Grandma, I love you to the moon and back, and we are reaching for you to make it to over 100 years old!

To My God Grandmother
Sandra

Thank you so much for being more than a best friend to my grandmother. She loved you more than you know. Also, thank you for adopting me as your granddaughter. I love our talks on the phone. You have helped me with my spiritual walk more than you know.

To Pastor & First Lady Handsom

To the Pastor and First Lady, thank you so much for your prayers and for always encouraging me to shoot for the stars and letting me know I am special. Thank you for being more than just pastor and first lady but family. I know I can depend on you and it does not matter what time of the night I call. You all have truly been a blessing to me and my family.

To My Hometown Swainsboro

I am excited to give my hometown, Swainsboro, the hope that you can make a big impact even if you are from a small town. God sends unlikely people to unlikely places to do unlikely things all the time for His glory!

To Pastor Marcus Gill

Dr. Marcus Gill, you and your ministry inspire me so much. I have been one of your greatest fans since I was in high school, and I am so grateful that God has allowed us to connect. You have achieved everything that I want to accomplish, such as becoming an author, artist, preacher, motivator, a college graduate with certification from Harvard, and traveling the world! Thank you for agreeing to do my foreword without hesitation. Thank you so much for believing in me and my ministry. You are a wonderful role model to me and the millions you reach daily.

To My Grandmother Dora

Dear Grandma Dora,

Grandma, you were the best to ever do it! I was your sunshine, and you were the light to my shine. I will never forget the times we spent together. You were a true diva, and thank you for teaching me how to dress. You didn't meet any strangers. We would have a church service with people anywhere literally. We used to have a church service with people in the bathroom, car, and restaurant. We would have it on the phone, the store, and at the hospital. You name it, we were there, and it didn't matter! You were the best cook! No one can cook that cube steak and homemade macaroni like you can. I have always been spoiled by you. Even if my parents said no, you would always give me a yes. That's why I'm too spoiled now! LOL. It's all your fault – shame on you!

I still can't believe it has been two years since you've been gone. Your death really caught me off guard. It's funny how doctors think they know how much time we have left, but only God knows. That shows doctors can't do anything without Him. When you died, it was a different kind of hurt – a hurt I cannot even explain. However, I find peace in knowing if God took you on, that it was for the best. Oh, how I wish you could see who I have become and will become.

You told me I would do great things at a young age in ministry. Oh, how I wish you were here to witness it. Wow, you missed me graduating with my Associate and Bachelor degrees with honors, like I told you, and my 20th, 21st, and 22nd birthdays. Yes, that was very different for me. Wow, you will not be able to see my ministry in the future or my wedding when that time comes, but that's okay. I choose to reflect on our happy times. I reflect on the times we sang and praised God together. I remember the many vacations we took. I reflect on how you spoiled me, lol. I will reflect on when you were there for my award ceremonies, high school graduation, and me winning the homecoming queen. I choose to reflect on the times we were twins and dressed like divas. I'm still a fashionista, and I have to represent you in style. I promised that your legacy would live on through me. I meant that, and it still stands true.

The thing I admire most about you, grandma, is how you touched all those lives in the hospital while you were critically ill. It really touched my heart when I saw the mass of nurses and doctors coming in and out of your room to check on you. All the nurses abandoned their hall because you touched them just that much. You were doing more work than many of those who are in perfectly good health. You were so selfless and always giving to others in your time of need. You really had a charm with that smile of yours. You were such an inspiration, and you have impacted the lives of many. Grandma, you truly fought the good fight of faith to the end! You don't have to suffer anymore. I know you look so beautiful in heaven being the diva that you are. God has truly smiled on you, and I know you are living your best life now!

I love you, and I promise to keep your legacy going. Until then, so long my dear grandmother. I promise to make you proud. I wish you were still here to see everything I will be. Everything I do from here on out is for you!

Foreword

by Marcus Gill

Life is beautiful. The only unfortunate thing about life is that as beautiful as it is, there are so many ugly seasons. The Truth be told, there is nothing that we can do about that. Jesus told us something in John chapter number 16 verse, number 33. He said, "in this world, we're going to have trials and tribulations." That means that no matter what, we are always going to have to deal with some type of trouble. Life has ups and downs, but the good news is trouble doesn't last always! God is with us through everything! As you read this book, Mikella will give much insight into what it means to persevere.

You know, God is so awesome in all of His ways. He'll see you going through a flood and won't let the waters overtake you. He'll see you going through the fire, but won't let the flames kindle against you! You could be going through the worst season of your life, and yet you'll come out with the victory! That's the joy of having a true relationship with the Most High God!

I've had some experiences in my life where I didn't know how I would come out. Let's be frank and honest; there are some seasons in my life where it got so bad that I had to ask if God even existed! Relationship problems, family problems, financial problems; all of these things were taking over my life and making it painful to carry. God is the only one who delivered me from my dark place! You must understand, even now, that your past did nothing but give you a testimony!

I always say that my past only prepared me for the prosperity of my now and future! Sometimes we just need to be thankful for the story that we have to tell. Be thankful for what God allowed in our lives. Be grateful for the fact that God has given you the ability to be sustained through the storm. It reminds me of the question that is asked of us in the word, "If God be for us, who can be against us?" As you're reading this book, you'll see that Mikella has been through the fire and the flood, but she made it out! Only God can do it! When you read her testimony, be reminded that if God delivered her, He can and will deliver you too!

When you make it through, it's going to be evident that the anointing is on your life. The pressure has a purpose. The trials come with a reward. I really believe this – that the more you go through, the more anointing you carry. You want the anointing. We don't always want to go through, but we want the anointing. All that you've been through or are going through now is just a pressing for the anointing!

It's your time! Go through life, knowing that you are covered.

Marcus Gill
Pastor, Author, Speaker

Introduction

WHO IS MIKELLA HANSLEY (SPEAKS) AND HOW DID THE MINISTRY COME ABOUT?

"If it were easy, everyone would do it".
-Tom Hanks-

Wow, I wrote my book at age 20, and now I am officially an author at the age of 22! To God be all the glory! I have self-published the first book of my series. When I tell you that God has been faithful, believe me! The number eight is the number of new beginnings and He has truly given me a new beginning in the last 8 years of my life (from 2012 to 2020). I was once the author of my own bad chapters. Now, I am the author of my first book that will help you to navigate through this thing we call life. I am the only child of Ministers Michael and Beatrice Hansley. My parents call me their "miracle baby" because they were unable to conceive for most of their married life together, but God had other plans and blessed them with me.

I am a speaker, educator, poet, singer, writer, and songwriter. Some call me a young preacher, young Esther, Hat Lady, a model, and sometimes just Kellz or Kella. I am just an ordinary small-town girl who is extremely passionate about Jesus. I have been in church since I was little (in my mother's womb lol), but I truly came to know Jesus for myself starting my freshman year of college.

I am God's workmanship and I have been placed on earth to bring glory to his name! I genuinely believe God designed me to be a world changer not for my glory but for His glory! I desire to encourage people to walk in their God given purpose so they can be happy and fulfilled! I hope my generation can experience God in the way that I have! It does not matter how you started or what you have done, because you can be redeemed. God Loves you so much and there is HOPE!

What excites me most about my future contribution to the kingdom is that my "Big God" will get all the glory and souls being saved! I love to boast on my God, and I cannot do anything without Him. He is my everything! In the word it tells us that we are God's workmanship (Ephesians 2:10) (Jeremiah 1:5). Everyone is here on earth to bring all the glory to him. It brings me joy to make people happy.

The ministry and speaking started out through my phone and social media. God placed it on my heart to turn it into a blog and book at the end of 2017. God had already dealt with me about writing a book in 2017, but he brought it back to my remembrance after the passing of my grandmother. After my grandmother passed, God put me in a place of isolation, and He showed me that I am called to Millennials, Generation Z, and women. My ministry and speaking platforms consist of a YouTube, blog, and social media outlets. I use Millennial for

Christ to encourage Millennials specifically. Mikella Speaks is used to encourage and educate everyone (especially Millennials and Generation Z). I have a group chat that empowers women. I am also known as Mikella Educates (Mikella's College Success Workshops), because I had the opportunity to graduate college early, debt-free, and with honors. I teach college success workshops (Internationally). These workshops are not only for students in high school but also for those in college. I want students to have access to the funds and resources they need to succeed. I am always speaking in some form, whether I am teaching, writing, motivating, or singing. That is how the name Mikella Speaks came about.

Many of the articles/passages you read in this book were already sent to my contacts or posted on my social media when I was 18 years old. I desire to spread and share the word of God with everyone! I hope my ministry will eventually go worldwide and be a part of churches (maybe even to be used as a guide or series for Bible study and college classes). My objective is to inspire and motivate Millennials and Generation Z to live an effective Christian life by teaching the principles of faith, wisdom, and purpose. I have an emphasis on those that are lost, hurt, confused, and in need of deliverance.

Through my ministry people have been delivered, had hurts healed, and have given testimonies of prevented suicide. Some are walking in faith and wisdom in areas of college, their Christian walk, and applying for and receiving jobs. While others are walking in their purpose in the areas of writing books and singing. I have had many defeats and many triumphs. I used to be a rebellious teen – a filthy rag saved by God's grace. I was headed down the wrong path, but God changed me. I want to exemplify God's grace as it has been shown to me. I want people to know that they are special, and God has a purpose for their lives. My goal is to give people hope despite their past or present circumstances. God is greater!

Millennials and Generation Z deal with so many issues, but the three I would like to focus on are acceptance, knowing God for themselves, and figuring out their purpose. Acceptance is a major issue for this generation. Oftentimes, there is not a paternal or maternal figure present in their life. This causes an identity crisis because they are not being guided by authority figures. They struggle with discipline and living holy because they so desire to be accepted. Because Millennials and Generation Z want to be accepted, they turn to many things such as sex, drugs, gang activity, and homosexuality. Not being accepted can lead to other issues such as depression and suicide. The pressure from these issues controls their mind, and they try to be perfect and compare their lives to others. The truth is we all struggle, and no one has a perfect life.

Many Millennials and Generation Z do not know God, so they settle for anything. Once they truly get to know God, they can develop that personal relationship and He will reveal their future and purpose to them (Jeremiah 29:11). I have put together this book series (from my personal experiences, quotes, scriptures, and activities) and it is structured in a unique way that includes strategies for mainly every issue Millennials and Generation Z may face. I want my life to be an example of hope to them.

I am not perfect by any means. I love my favorite artist Jonathan McReynolds because he is real and an imperfect human being. I love his ministry and singing because he focuses on imperfections. He has a quote that I absolutely love, and it says, "Shame made me feel like I had to be perfect, but I'm slowly shedding the need water and I shot up out of it quickly, powerfully, and supernaturally. The water was in a huge tube that looked like it could have been sixty feet deep. In real life, the devil TRIED to drown me but it didn't work! The day I had this dream was interesting. I have a friend and told them about it, and it gave them the confirmation they needed to do what God was telling them to do. Not only was the dream confirming that I was about to go through a storm and that God would bring me through it powerfully, but it was also a confirmation to what he was doing in my friend's life. In John 7:38 the Bible says, "He that believeth on me, as the scripture hath said, out of his belly shall flow rivers of living water". What this scripture means, is that the promises that God has made are still true. It is in Jesus (the living water) that we will have everything we need(especially emphasizing the Holy Spirit) to survive and thrive. We as believers will have amazing testimonies to tell and share about the glory of God. In this book, you will see many ways that God has performed signs, miracles, and wonders in my life.

I realized in 2019, that my books would not only align with my ministry, but also with my speaking career as a Christian motivational speaker. This book is a 20-day guide based on my life journey/testimony and how I overcame hardships while being perfected at the same time. One thing I realized is that we all have a gift, but what you are anointed to do will prevail over your imperfections.

I started the book in May 2018 but began writing between June and July by way of my blog/testimony. I had 40 sections in my guide, and I condensed it to 20 because God showed me it would be a series. In July of 2018, my life changed forever. God helped me to realize that I was not perfect, and I didn't have to be. In November of 2018 until May 2019, I was broken down. It was not until God broke me, and showed me my imperfections through my brokenness, that I realized I had power and that I was anointed. This book, "Anointing Over Perfection: The Power of Perseverance in Pursuit Of Purpose" was inspired by me looking at all the mistakes I've made in my life, feeling/being broken, and not feeling qualified to be used by God. However, God still chose me anyway.

As a matter of fact, throughout the Bible, the main people God used were really messed up and had serious issues. My favorite man in the Bible is David. David was a man who loved God with his whole heart, yet he committed adultery and committed murder. None of these things stopped David from going to heaven or walking in his purpose. David was God's chosen vessel, and his anointing and purpose were greater than his imperfections. I'm not saying that you should or have permission to sin on purpose. I'm not saying that you will not have consequences, but what I would like to convey to you is there is hope for redemption and restoration. I realized that no matter what happened to me in life, or how I responded to what happened to me in life, God would not stop loving me. God is going to use everything I went through for His glory.

My grandmother Dora died in March 2018. She was a strong believer in Jesus Christ. Before she passed, I promised that her legacy would live on through me. My ministries are one way of keeping my word to my grandma. It is because of her and my parents' teachings that I am wise beyond my years and excelling in different aspects of my life.

God placed it on my heart to write a book. The writing idea was not of me at all. If I am honest, God had to isolate me and force me to write it. My book is a guide filled with strategies and techniques to help people to walk in wisdom, faith, and into their God-given purpose by looking at the imperfections and trials in my life. Know that I am very transparent, and I give personal testimonies of how I made it through difficulties in my life.

I was trying to figure out my purpose, trying to get rid of bad habits and find a positive project. I asked God to make sense of the difficult situations I was experiencing in my life, and that is when he told me to write the book. I said I do not know how to publish or self-publish, no one in my immediate family has written a book, and I do not have the money. I felt like my life needed to be perfect before I could write a book. I figured I should have my law degree, career, be married, etc. God told me He wanted to inspire people by my imperfections, and just by all the things I have achieved this far. He told me that I would have a series, and people would be able to see me continuously growing and blessed. He told me I did not have time to waste because some young people need to read this book right now. I am way more transparent than I would like to be in this book, but God said to write, so that is what I did! He told me, "Daughter, you asked for a positive project. You asked me to make sense of your life. Just write, and I will handle the rest." I said, "Okay God" and He gave me the format for my book, and I began to write on July 12, 2018. I was still in the process of writing the book (and almost finished) one Sunday, the minister at my church said 'silence your spirit and listen to God'. I heard God as clear as day say, "Stop worrying my daughter. I am working everything for your good. Keep your focus on me. I *am* working everything for your good." After that day, I again said, "Okay, God, I trust You" and my joy began to come back. Shortly after, everything began to fall in place.

In the Bible perfect means *to mature,* and I have truly grown in God. That is why Psalm 138:8 is the guiding verse for my ministry. I call myself "the evolving motivator" because I haven't arrived, but I'm on my way! I truly believe the Lord will perfect what concerns you and truly establish you. I had to be imperfect to realize I was anointed, and I had to persevere to walk in my purpose.

Anointed means *set aside for a holy use of some sort.* What you're anointed to do will always be greater than the gift itself; the anointing is your purpose. The imperfections and the perseverance in my life had to take place for God to perfect my life by pushing me into my purpose. Walking in God's will and purpose does not mean a perfect life without any troubles. You will have many troubles, but God's anointing on your life will bring you through. In this book, you will see that you can be successful and walk in purpose despite your imperfections if you only endure! Yes, I have struggled, but I never quit! Remember, the race is not given to the swift nor to the strong, but to the one that keeps on pressing until the race is won (Ecclesiastes 9:11).

Significant Dates

In July 2018, my life changed forever, and I began to walk in my purpose. July 2020 marks two years of ministry. This is the exact month I wrote the first five chapters of my book.

November 18 is a significant date for me. On **November 18, 2017**, I wrote a journal excerpt that is included as sneak peek for my next book. It is located at the end of the book. That was my first attack. As you read the section titled, "Fighting for My Life", you will see I was attacked on this day again in 2018. I've realized that when God is doing something major in your life the timing is specific and the attacks are a sign of the blessing soon to come.

November 26 is a significant date for me. I wrote the following in my journal:

November 26, 2017

Trusting In God Even When You Cannot Hear Him

I am currently a college student. My whole college career has been a faith walk from scholarships to my involvement. I am trying to make a big decision – what college I would like to transfer to. I am also trying to figure out how I will finance it. To some people, this is not a big deal, but for me, it is. I am a woman after God's own heart, and I want my life to please Him. That means I want every aspect of my life to be in His will. I'm also in a place where I am trying to grow in God and figure out what my purpose is. He has been showing me bits and pieces but not the whole picture.

I am the type of person who likes to know the ins and outs of everything. I am a planner, and I like things organized and for all my paths to be mapped out. What is my final destination, and why am I going through this and that? Why can't I hear you? I'm confused, and I realize I can't make it on my own. God told me, "My daughter, as you praise Me and spend worship time with Me, I'll direct your path." The Bible says a good man's steps are ordered by God. I may not know my full purpose yet, but I'm not panicking. I'm going through this season being still and knowing that He is God. I understand we are all created to tell others about God and His unfailing love. Be encouraged, my sisters and brothers. Even when God has not shown you your entire purpose, know that you are right where you need to be. To everything, there is a time and season. We go through everything for a reason and not by coincidence. Pick your head up and praise God for what He is doing in advance! Don't give up, because you have made it too far!

November 26, 2018, is significant because I went through the biggest trial in my life thus far. That is when I realized the power and anointing that God had bestowed upon my life. This season of my life changed me forever.

November 26, 2019

On this day, I went into a vision. In it, a prophet that I know in real life appeared and said, "You are going to go viral." After hearing those words, the vision ended.

November 26, 2020

Glory to God! This day is so special to me because this is the release date of the book "three" years later. I've found myself, and I'm walking in God's will and purpose for my life three years later. I have been through much the last eight years of my life. 2020 is my year of new beginnings, and God is perfecting my life.

PART I

The Vision

Covered By Three: The Vision (March 14, 2019)

This book is dedicated to my grandmother and parents!

The
CB3
Triple
Anointing
Revelation
April 23, 2020
Father, Son, Holy Spirit
Faith, Wisdom, Purpose
Grandma, Father, Mother
Anchored, Aligned, Assigned
Ministry, Education, Motivation
Millennials, Generation Z, Women

The holy spirit will make intercession!
It took me three years in all to come to this revelation!

The Covered By Three Vision

On March 14, 2019, God gave me the vision for Covered by Three sitting in the church at an appreciation on a Thursday night. I noticed that my parents and I were sitting in a triangle form, and I began to think about how we function when we are working together. I was behind them, and they were in front of me sitting, three seats apart, and together we made a triangle shape.

It seemed as if I represented faith, and my parents represented the Holy Spirit and purpose. When I think about myself being an only child and having two parents, I had faith to depend on them to teach me wisdom and faith to be successful in life. It works the same way in the spiritual. In each one of my videos, you will hear me giving you wisdom, applying faith, and demonstrating purpose (me making the videos is me walking in my purpose). The Trinity works together to help us to be successful, prosperous, live right, and walk into our God-given purpose. The three must work together!

. . .

There are a few more things that are significant about Covered by Three. God had me to write out my life testimony around July in 2017, which was three years ago. As you read under my significant dates, I was trying to figure out my purpose on November 26, 2017. Not only am I releasing my first book now three years later on that specific date, but I also know my purpose and I have knowledge on my triple anointing. I had two prophets relay the same message to me. Both told me to pray three times a day because my ministry is bigger than I know and that God is raising me up to be a great leader. When I was in South Africa on September 21, 2019, I received the first prophecy. As soon as I came back to the United States on September 29, 2019, my God Mom Cubia told me the same thing and confirmed it. The funny thing is that neither one of these women knew each other. I'm so thankful and grateful for my God Mom encouraging me to do and be my best in my ministry, especially before I went to Africa and since I came back. I am also so very thankful to Aunt Pam for always being there for me, introducing me to the scholarship director, and sharing the South Africa scholarship application with me. I love how God uses people to help lead you into purpose.

On March 29, 2020, God told me he wanted his people to be anchored, aligned, and assigned. Being anchored is having your faith deeply rooted in God and a one-on-one relationship with God. Being aligned is planting God's holy word in your heart and letting the Holy Spirit lead, guide, and make intercession on your behalf. The assignment is walking in the instructions and purpose that God gives you!

The Reasoning Behind Covered By Three

First, you are covered by God. He created you, and He is everything (John 1:1-5, Hebrews 11:6). There is only one God! He has all power, and he is omniscient and omnipresent! You must have "faith" in God First. Second, you are covered by the Holy Spirit because he is your "daily" guide. The Holy Spirit is your guide, "wisdom", and truth (John 16:13, Acts 1:8, Romans 8:26-27, Proverbs 3:5-6). Third, you are covered by the Son of God, Jesus (John 10:30). Because your sins and everything you would have to go through was taken care of when he died on the cross (John 3:16). His life was an example of "purpose" with the help of his Heavenly Father God and the Holy Spirit. Jesus is the flesh version and perfect representation of God (John 1:14, 1 Corinthians 8:6, John 11:25). That is the way that Covered by Three functions.

The reasoning behind Covered by Three is that you must first have faith to believe that God is God, and believe that Jesus Christ died on the cross for your sins. You must have faith in Him before you can walk in wisdom. You have to have faith to believe in the wisdom that God gives from His word (Proverbs 3:16). When you accept and learn wisdom from the Bible and Holy Spirit, you will be guided on when and how to step out on faith. After you have applied faith and wisdom, then you are equipped with all of the tools needed to walk into your God given purpose!

The purpose is faith and wisdom combined. When you get wisdom from God, He shows you your calling. Jesus' life is a perfect example of purpose, I and many Bible scholars believe that he completed a major part of his purpose in three years. He applied His faith and wisdom throughout his life as an example to us. The Holy Spirit that dwelled in Jesus is the same Holy Spirit that dwells in us. Once He shows you your calling, He will then give you the steps to walk in your purpose through bits and pieces. I truly believe God can give you a triple blessing!

Reasoning Behind Logo Design
(I WANT YOU TO NOTICE THERE ARE THREE SECTIONS TO MY LOGO DESIGN)

The Abbreviations

The CB3 stands for Covered By Three and MFC stands for Millennial For Christ.

Shapes

The three triangles represent the trinity, my triple anointing, and what Covered By Three is all about. The triangles are also in the shape of the letter M to represent the first initial of my name, Mikella. The microphone represents the speaking and singing aspects of my brand. The pencil inside of the microphone represents the educational aspect of my brand.

Colors

The colors black, red, and white have always been my favorite colors before I even knew their meanings. In Christianity, black represents darkness and uncleanliness. When you come into the light of Jesus, your sins are washed in His red blood (which also represents his protection) and you become white as snow. The color black also represents power, authority (leadership), and success. The color red is known as a representation of fire, so it is associated with energy, strength, power, determination as well as passion, desire, and love. The color white stands for hope, purity, mental clarity, impartiality, and organization. It's so amazing how each color represents my personality and the aspects and principles of Covered By Three.

Every part of the logo was carefully thought out, and the ideas were given to me directly from God for his purpose and glory.

Trademark and Copyrights of this design belongs to Mikella Hansley 2020

The Triple Anointing

On April 23, 2020, God revealed to me personally that I am covered by three. Not only did God reveal this to me, but He also had four prophets to confirm this. I am covered under the anointing of my mother, father, and grandmother. They are the three people in my life that I have spent the most time with, and they instilled the principles of God in me. As the only child, everything falls on me.

I am called to minister, motivate, and educate. God also told me I am specifically called to Millennials (college students), Generation Z (college students), and Women (the fashion part is for women, but I plan to make a few pieces for men as well). I am multi-gifted and anointed, and God revealed to me that Generational curses and limitations are breaking through me.

God told me he has called me to Millennials, and he told me not to worry about the fact that it was not my specific age group (1

Timothy 4:12, Psalm 8:2). He told me that he would use me to even relate to those who are close to my age group and older. He told me they, too, need what I have. God also has called me Generation Z, because that is my specific generation, and people who are my age will see me as an example. He also showed me that I would be a role model to many women, in the fact that I am a woman that has been able to achieve success in many areas of my life. I specifically desire for women to know how to love themselves, find themselves, and hold their emotions together without a husband. God called me to people in college in all three of these age categories, because I have had much success in college, and I have information to share with many.

God gave me the revelation that everything that my mom, father, and grandmother were not able to do on the level they desired, I would do. My grandmother had a prophetic gift, the gift of encouraging others, speaking in tongues, songwriting, preaching, and she was an intercessor. I, too, have these gifts. My grandmother, up to the day of her death, prayed for me to walk in my purpose. I always knew I would be a speaker of some sort, because I've always loved to talk and sing as a little girl. My uncle nicknamed me "talking stomach." Growing up, talking used to be the only thing I would get in trouble for in school (haha). She would always tell my mother, "Sunshine is going to be alright and she is going to do a special great work for the Lord." In March of 2018, in my psychology class, I had to write down what I thought I would be doing in the future. Also, on February 24, 2018 I wrote in my journal that I believe God is calling me to be a Christian motivational speaker, because I'm always encouraging people. On the paper, I wrote that I could be a motivational speaker. Now, I wish that my grandmother could see me and all that I've accomplished between years of 2018 and 2020. I never expected to make it this far at a young age but she always told me at a young age, that I would be prominent for singing, speaking, and preaching, and I would always be like, "yeah right, grandma," but deep down, I've always felt it was true. I eventually expressed to her that I knew it was true. My grandmother desired to write books and travel around the world, and the glory is unto God that I have achieved these things. Not only have I done these things, but I plan to publish a book from her journal. Lastly, she had a really great fashion sense, and so do I. I hope to have my own fashion business eventually.

2020 marks three years that my parents have been ordained as ministers. My father, preaches, has the gift of tongues, sings, writes songs, and he is an intercessor. He has produced songs and CDs in the studio, and I, too, can do all these things. My mother is a very intelligent woman. She was the salutatorian of her graduating class. Everyone thought she would be most successful. She received her Associate's degree, but she had to drop out of college her last year due to being very ill. I am smart like her, and it was always her desire for me to graduate from college. She is also a preacher, teacher, motivator, intercessor, songwriter, has a prophetic gift, and she speaks in tongues as well. I, too, have the gifts my mother has. I have obtained my Bachelor's Degree with honors, early, and debt-free. I have had the opportunity to use my education for God's glory in my country and internationally by teaching college success workshops.

In her battle with sickness, my grandmother taught me the importance of having faith, no matter what. My father taught me as a little girl to never be wise in my own eyes. My dad emphasized the principle of wisdom in me by challenging me to read Proverbs every day. My mother emphasized to me daily that God had a plan for my life. She encouraged me to walk in wisdom and purpose.

PART II

Truth

.

Can You Imagine?!

Can you imagine having to watch your grandmother suffer for two years (really more but intensified in that time frame)?

Can you imagine your whole life-changing in a week and a half after the doctor told you your grandmother had more time to live?

Can you imagine watching and hearing your grandma (very last words to you) saying, "I can't breathe" and is immediately put on life support?

(Mind you, she just died the night before and was resuscitated, and you really thought that she was going to make it.)

. . .

Can you imagine one day before she dies hugging you, and she cries and tries her hardest to mouth the word "sunshine"? (Cause remember she can't talk anymore.)

Can you imagine your father getting off a phone call and then tells you that your grandmother has died? All you can feel is numbness inside while desperately wanting to scream on the outside.

Can you imagine how it feels to lose your best friend, queen, and spiritual partner all in one? It's kind of a hard feeling to explain the only word I can think of is PAIN. This really broke my heart! This isn't fair! Why me!?!

Can you imagine crying (and crying) yourself to sleep at night cause that's all you can really do, right?

Can you imagine replaying it in your mind over and over saying, "I just want my granny back!"

I remember the prophet came to me and said it is okay to let her go.

But how do you just let go of something so very dear!?!

. . .

It's not that easy, and sometimes it's fear!

Sometimes writing it out like this helps me to cope!

Why can't this just be over! Why isn't this just a joke?

This feeling in my heart, sometimes I wish I weren't sober!

Then maybe I wouldn't feel all this pain.

Then maybe I wouldn't feel so drained.

Then maybe, just maybe then, all this anxiety will go away!

I didn't write this for you to feel sorry for me.

I wrote this so you can see that it's only been God's grace carrying me.

When you depend on God, only He can heal your heart.

It's only God that can keep you from falling apart.

· · ·

Maybe I did fall apart, but God changed my heart.

When you depend on God, He will give you a brand new start.

Unspoken
THE UNTOLD TRUTH OF MY LIFE

God Was Calling Me and His Hands On Me Even at a Young Age

I once heard a saying, "Don't just read my first chapter, read my whole story". Marvin Sapp wrote a song that says, "So glad I made it! I made it." He went on to say, "So if you see me cry, it's just a sign that I'm still alive. I got some scars, but I'm still alive in spite of the calamity. He still has a plan for me. It's working for my good, and it's building my testimony."

In the year of 2017, my cousin asked me to come and speak to the youth at his event, and I pondered in my mind what I could talk about. As a spirit led believer, I began to seek God about it. I began to write out my testimony and the word perseverance came to my mind. God told me I would have the opportunity to share my testimony with many young people. I want you to notice that number three again. It is now three years later than

I'm sharing my story, because that event was cancelled in 2017. My story is now in my own book.

Just because I am young does not mean I have not had any sleepless nights. I have faced many difficulties in my life. God told me I need to write out my story and share it. I began to seek God about it, and He gave me the word perseverance. Perseverance is the steadfastness in doing something despite difficulty or delay in achieving success. Perseverance is not giving up. It is persistence and tenacity, the effort required to do something, and keep doing it till the end – *even* if it's hard. Vocabulary.Com states, "perseverance originally comes from the Latin *perseverantia* and means to abide by something strictly." When I was a little girl learning how to ride a bicycle, my father always told me to persevere. I've always applied what he taught me in my natural walk, but I later realized that I needed perseverance for my spiritual walk as well; I have to persevere in prayer, fasting, faith, reading the word, hearing the word, and going to church.

My mother was barren and was not supposed to have a child. While carrying me, she was very sick, so much so that she had to be put on bed rest. My mama almost had a miscarriage in the first few months of carrying me. She had tried for years to have a child, and I thank God that she did not give up. She did not have me until she was thirty-one years old. While she was pregnant they told her to abort me because the test showed that I would have a central nervous system disorder that would affect me greatly. She decided to carry me anyway. After that came delivery time. During this process, they thought I would die because my mother's sugar was too high, and mine was too low. That was not the case. I was choking myself, and they had to get me out immediately.

At the age of three, I choked on peppermint and almost died. God intervened with my aunt, placed strategically at this event. She performed the Heimlich maneuver on me and saved my life.

I knew from a young age that God had put something in me when my teachers in pre-k and kindergarten would pay me to quote the scriptures. I also knew when I got convicted in my spirit for three months for watching a secular music video. God had me sensitive to evil spirits at a young age. As a matter of fact, the person who sang the song came out about a pact she made with the enemy. I cried and was depressed for all three months just because of my conviction. My parents knew then too.

I went through a series of seeing angels in my room at night in the form of a man. One day in church, as my father was teaching Sunday school, I saw big angel wings behind him. That was a sign of the glory of God. These things all happened to me at a young age. It is at a young age that I began to walk in the supernatural.

My Life, Growing Up, and High School

The devil really desired to take me out growing up. I suffered from severe allergies, chronic bronchitis, and asthma. I eventually grew out of those illnesses. In the sixth grade, on Halloween night, I had a critical blockage, and the doctor admitted me and scheduled me for surgery the next morning. The surgeon came in the next morning, and he said, "I don't see anything, you probably just have food poisoning." I was treated for food poisoning and then released. However, to this day I believe God gave me supernatural healing. After that, I dealt with severe kidney issues. I went from physician to physician and none of them could target what was wrong with me. One day God healed me, and the issues stopped. God is a healer and is truly amazing.

For most of my life, my mother was gravely ill. It was so hard growing up never knowing if my mom was going to die. She's had more surgeries than I can count on my two hands! I remember many times laying at her bedside saying, "God, please don't let my mother die!" My mother should have died many years ago, but God said not so. My mother and I know that *truly* God is a miracle worker.

Growing up, I was bullied. I couldn't fit in, no matter how hard I tried. I could never understand why I had to go through that. I did not do anything to anybody. I later found out they were jealous of me and that I was anointed. I just wanted to come to school and make good grades. It got to the point that I did not want to go to school. I began to skip school. The students would pick on me every day. I mean *every day* about anything – my eyes, being a church girl, my hair (I used to have extremely long hair, but it fell out terribly from a bad perm), clothes, and looks. They even picked on me for being smart. I used to make myself look dumb because I felt like I was too smart.

I used to get so angry with my parents. I started rebelling against them because they were so strict on me, and I felt like that was why I was being bullied. I was angry at my sheltered life. To the adults reading, my hope for you is to know that although your child may be rebelling right now, know that God can change them. I am a living witness. However, I now know my parents just wanted what was best for me.

Because my parents were ministers and very strict, my peers knew I was not going to fight back. I was so weak back then. I remember a time a girl took my hand (she was way bigger than me) and she slapped this girl's face. That girl's face that she hit was almost three times bigger than me. The girl slung me everywhere and hit me all upside the head and I had bruises and all. One day, I had a stye in my eye, and many people lied on me and said I was beaten up. I was so sad about this. One time I was beaten up in the bathroom. Some girls kicked me and pulled my hair. I was bullied so bad that my mother was up there every other day trying to get them to do something about it, but they never did. I asked God how long I have to go through this and why can't I just go to another school (like a private school).

Most people in my grade did not like me, and that is what made it even worse. They would make me feel like I was nothing, and I had such low self-esteem. It even came to the point that I contemplated suicide, but God! I wanted to fit in because I was an only child, and I was very lonely. Also, I was just tired of being bothered. Also, I did not really know who I was in Christ. My peers used to hit me and gang up on me. They would drag me by my hair and call me all kinds of names. They would tell lies to me to the teacher and try to get me in trouble. They also would make up really mean rumors about me, and people would believe them. When I used to ride the bus, they would throw spitballs on me. My black peers would say I act like a white person because I was intelligent, talked proper, and was trying to make something of myself.

Once I went to camp for JROTC, and a lot of girls ganged up on me because a boy (who they thought was the finest) wanted to talk to me. In reality, he was trying to talk to everybody, but I guess I was supposed to be the main one. Eventually, they moved me into a room by myself at camp. Many females hated me and did not like me because their men were trying to talk to me, and I did not even want their men. The sad thing is I was almost suspended because of their foolishness. I had to be placed in honors classes in my first year of high school, out of my will, just so my classmates could leave me alone.

A lot of students did not like me because my mother worked for the school system. I was also in a lot of honor positions in high school, and the students would disrespect me. They thought that I had favor and received special treatment. Not the case! I worked very hard, and my teachers noticed that about me, and that is why I was nominated for so many awards.

I had always taken my academics seriously until I made it to the ninth grade. In ninth grade, I started to rebel against my parents and those in authority, and I also experienced a decline in grades. When I made it to the ninth grade being smart wasn't really considered cool. I took a math class, and I would walk in there every day and fuss with the teacher and go to sleep. Guess where that got me – an F. You see I desperately wanted to fit in because I was bullied. I had a loving family, yet still rejected. I rebelled because this world could not satisfy me. My mom took me to the police station, not inside just outside during my rebellious life to put fear in me and show me where disobedient people end up. At that moment, I was shaken. However, I still continued to be rebellious a little while longer, but I thank my mom for that. She cared enough and loved me enough to say, "Hey, you don't want to end up like these people." She didn't want me to end up being a statistic. She knew I was a leader. She knew I was great.

I had to retake my math class, and that was a wakeup call for me. I took the class again, and I made an A. Not only did I make an A in that class, but I also decided from that point on to be a leader. I had to work hard and had many sleepless nights because my second year of high school, I was determined to get back in honors classes and make an A average in them. The funny story is I hid in the bathroom when they announced honors graduate because I wasn't sure I was going to receive it. They had to text my mother to find me. She texted me to tell me to go into the auditorium because they were looking for me. It felt so good to receive so many accolades and obtain honor graduate status throughout the rest of my years of high school. I want you to know that the girl you know today has not been perfect. The woman you see today is just a filthy rag that was saved by God's grace.

I joined JROTC and became a mature and intelligent leader. God used JROTC to change my life. When I would do interviews, I would do so well that people would say it must have been proper training through the JROTC Program. My sergeant would always tell me that I was great. He would always tell me if it were easy then everyone would do it. Now I see everything he

27

was talking about. I see it clearly now. JROTC made me a leader. It challenged me mentally and physically. It changed my behavior and every aspect of my life. Many people could see the difference. It taught me discipline and hard work. It taught me how to be a good citizen and how to treat people. It gave me a sense of belonging. That is how it is when we come is the family of God. Having a relationship with God makes your whole life better.

I love how God works and how He uses things I went through in my life to help me in ministry. Besides failing a class in high school, I experienced heartbreak. The guy broke up with me and didn't even tell me why until three months later. However, that made things worse, but at the same time, I had a sense of closure. When I found out why it brought more questions to mind, and I needed more closure. It's hard enough to cope when you know why. He just broke up with me, and I knew I did nothing wrong. That was my first love, and that experience was so painful that I can't even explain. I could have dealt with it better if I had known why. I experienced the heartbreak of my last semester of school. During this time, I was working at a pillow factory, struggling in my honors pre-calculus class, and trying to figure out what school I would go to next and how I can pay for it. Also, I was sick during my last semester of high school. I had bronchitis, a sinus infection, and an ear infection. After I experienced this heartbreak (and was still dealing with all those other things), I wanted to give up (See Sneak Peek on pg. 139). It hurt the most because it was a few weeks before prom, and I had already purchased everything. Through praying and pressing on through my circumstances, everything worked out! I completed my job, and I passed my pre-calculus class with a B. God is faithful.

My College Journey

Now fast forward to college. I was so happy when I started college because I was like now, I can make up for everything I thought I had missed out on. I used to try to fit in by going to parties, but I felt so out of place. For example, when I won homecoming queen, and I was at the party they tried to make me dance and I was like, "No, I'm good."

Those things they did to me and called me in high school had gotten in my spirit. I didn't get free until my third year of college, and it was *so hard*. My freedom came through writing this book, which made me very uncomfortable because I had to dig down really deep into my past. I tried to brush over and act like all the things never happened. God told me I could not be effective for the kingdom if I was angry and in bondage to my past. He told me that my past and what happened to me did not define me nor hinder the blessings that He has for me in the future. On August 24, 2018, I wrote this in my blog:

"Tonight, at the women's conference the woman who preached did not want to preach what God was telling her to preach because it ran so deep. She said God never told her to do that before. I know she was telling the truth because I have a discerning spirit, and I watched her wrestle with that thing until she stood up and finally began to preach it. However, I am so glad she obeyed God because that message was just for me. Literally, the same thing she went through is very similar to what I went and was going through. I started not to even go because I had so much homework but it was ordained by God. The moral of my story is to obey God because he blesses others through your obedience".

. . .

That night was confirmation for me that I did need to write this book and share it.

Before achieving my Associate's degree with Cum Laude Honors, I had many trials and tribulations. My first obstacle was trying to get a scholarship. I applied for a scholarship that would have covered everything for me, and well, I didn't get it. I continued to apply for other scholarships, and I received some, and some I didn't. One day, I received a phone call telling me I had received a scholarship that would cover my full-tuition. Get this – I had not applied for this scholarship, and I was the only one at this university to receive the scholarship. I believe I was chosen because of my previous applications, but I truly know God did it!

During my first year of college, I backslid. I felt like my favorite artist Jonathan McReynolds when he said, "Lord, I'm split in two. Part of me loves the world and the other loves you. So, what do I do? I want to be saved, but I got to stay cool too." I fell in love with his music when I heard this song on BET in 2012.

You see, I know I had a call, but I did not want to walk in my purpose because I felt like that was not cool. I wanted to fit in, I did not want to stand out. I struggled with desperately wanting to fit in because of my sheltered lifestyle in high school. I wanted to experience something new. I felt like I had missed out on something. So, I tried going to the club, but I did not like it. The smoke almost took my breath, and there was no way I was going to dress in skimpy or indecent clothing like the other girls. It was so funny; I was classy at the club. When I was there, I was like a fish out of water – so out of place, especially considering that I can not dance. While I was in the club, I was like, "God what am I doing here? Please get me out of here!" I tried these things that my parents had been trying to protect me from all along. After doing so, I realized I had not missed out on anything at all. I was imagining things in my head and being influenced by my peers, who were making things out to be more than they really were. After that, I tried dating guys that my parents told me not to date. I wanted to do my own thing, and I was played by most of them. I was immature and trying to fill voids and ignore hurts that only God could fill and heal.

It was the summer of my first year of college that I became very serious about God and truly walking into my purpose. For a long time, I was not perfect. None of us are. Overall, I was doing the right things, following the commandments, and realizing what God wanted me to do in life, and then, my grandmother died. I literally watched her die right in front of me. I became angry with God because I felt like He had forsaken me. Plus, I had received a word about my husband a year and a few months ago, and I was like, "God why can't I just be married already. God, I am doing all the right things, and now you allow all this to happen!" So, I backslid again. However, I came back to God sooner this time. It *really* felt wrong. I told myself that God has brought me too far and that He has a purpose for my pain.

Okay, now onto the second obstacle. During my very first semester, my mother's best friend (my God aunt) died, and that was very heartbreaking. After that, not one, but both of my grandmothers *and* my mother were in the hospital all at one time. They were all hospitalized an hour and 30 minutes away from where I live. They were all in critical situations, so my father and

I would go up there every day. It was physically and spiritually draining. Throughout all of this, I remained faithful to my church, leadership positions on campus, and my academics. I had this one club adviser who gave me a very hard time through all I was going through. She almost made me quit, but I'm glad that my God was my strength. I fulfilled every obligation I was given.

Another issue was that I didn't have a car, but I thank God that I have dedicated parents who took me to every event. Also, my mother had a very threatening illness and we had to go back and forth to the hospital.I still remember sitting at the foot of her hospital bed crying again, "God please don't take my mother," because she was just that sick.

My mother and grandmother were both very ill my whole college career, and that is a lot to go through. Sometimes, my grandma and my mother would be sick at the same time. It's crazy that I spent most of my time at the hospital during my first two years of college. Like, I looked through old pictures and seen myself in a hospital with my family and said, "gosh I spent a lot of time there." My grades were even affected by it in my first semester of college.

The Breaking and the Vision

The last major obstacle I faced was my last month of the semester, about four weeks before graduating with my Associate's degree. My grandmother became very ill. She was already sick, and we were traveling back and forth every other week, back to back the whole two years while I was in college. She had been sick a while, and I watched my mother during her time of sickness neglect herself to take care of my grandmother. I also watched her cry for many days. I cried about the situation for many days as well. The first week before my grandmother's death we received a call saying she fell out of her wheelchair and hit the concrete. The same week I remember having to go to the hospital at 3:00 a.m. She had went into cardiac arrest and had to be resuscitated. I remember that day very well because I was inducted into the honor society that night. That did not kill her. A few days later, she had to be put on life support. I was sitting right there when she said, "I can't breathe." Being the Christian woman that I am I held onto my faith, and I kept going to school. Then, the day came when she was gone. When I received the news, I wanted to go on too. I knew she was dying, and I honestly thought I was prepared for it, but I'm here to tell you I wasn't.

Journal Entry
Date: 03/29/2018

Today was the last day that I saw my grandma alive in person. I was able to sing to her and have church with her one more time. Today I was the only person my grandma responded to. I hugged her and said, "Grandma, this is sunshine" and her heart rate went from 80 to 100. After that, she said "sunshine" and then she started crying like she didn't want to leave me and I started crying. I hated seeing her suffer and I know she wanted to stay here with me desperately. However, deep in my spirit I feel it is her time to go.

. . .

If I just am honest, I became angry with God. The heartbreak I experienced and watching my mother and other grandma suffer was enough. "How could she survive the last two times, but not this one, God? How could you take something else away from me that I value? God, she was my best friend." I had so much faith, and I prayed and prayed. I also fasted. At this point, I felt like God had forsaken me. I would try to go to school, and I would have to drive myself home, so I can have a meltdown because all I was having were flashbacks of her in the hospital bed where she was crying and called me Sunshine for the last time.

Shortly after my grandmother died, God took me into a vision. In the vision, I went down into some very deep water. I am talking like sixty feet deep. In the vision, I came out of the water so powerful and quickly. I figured it was God showing me that I will get through my grandmother's death. God told me that was not the only thing it represented. I am going to share the rest of my testimony and get back to that.

I went into extreme depression and my grades I had worked all hard to achieve the whole semester began to decline. Not only did I experience depression, but I was also affected physically. I was so stressed, and I cried so much that my eyes began to twitch. I started taking a sleep aid every night just to go to sleep at night. I was not a drinker, but I decided to go to the club and have a drink. Still, nothing changed. After that, I decided to get drunk one time, and the Holy Spirit told me not to do it, but I did it anyway. I had the presence of mind to call my mother to come to get me because if she had not come, I do not know what would have happened. Getting drunk did not help, and I was really messed up. The next week I was driving, and the Holy Spirit told me not to get on a certain highway, but I did it anyway. Boom! I got into a wreck, but I survived. This wreck was so scary and could have been detrimental because both cars were totaled.

After all, this happened since 2018, I found myself mourning over the holidays. At first, I was sad about not having a husband. Then it went to me being sad about not having a grandmother. During the whole process, I felt like I did not have one friend. If I am honest, I desired to be married. Especially after receiving the word about the great man I will marry. I was also upset because I did not have the funds to go to the school I desired to go to after receiving my Associate's. I applied for twenty-one scholarships, and I did not receive one. Plus, I was upset that I had paid a $120 fee that I could not get back. I worked so hard just to receive no after no. That was why I made all these decisions because I felt like I did not have anything to be happy or live for. I also felt like even though I finally made the decision to live right, and situations in my life were still going left. I even thought to myself, "What's the point of living right if I'm still getting undesired outcomes?"

After that, I contemplated committing suicide by overdose, but I never went through with it. I almost lost my mind, but God. The only thing that kept me from doing it was looking over my life and seeing how far God had brought me and remembering the promises He gave me. Also, people sending me messages about how much they were inspired by me and wanting to be like me kept me. I also remember how my grandmother had six heart attacks and had to be resuscitated three times. That reassured me because I know God is a miracle-working God, but it was just her time. I continued to praise God as hard as I could, and I also know that someone was praying for me. God invested too much into me for me to give up.

The Prayer Request and the Beginning of My Journey

I asked God to make sense of this difficult time in my life, and He did just that. He told me to start my blog, gave me a song (that is yet to be produced), and told me to write this book. God also placed in my heart to start a YouTube channel to go along with my movement *Millennial for Christ*. My breakthrough really came when I made my YouTube video "Get out your feelings. It's not what you see". After that, I wrestled just a little more, and I really got free when I made my YouTube video "Let Go of the Old. It's A New Season". In this video, I said, "weeping may endure for a night, but joy comes in the morning". After this video, I was truly set free. I let go and decided to not let depression hold me any longer. By the grace of God, I brought my grades up, and I ended the semester strong, making the Dean's List and therefore, still graduating with honors. Throughout my first two years of college, I received many accolades and honors.

The Final Straw (Spiritual Warfare, See Page 141)

While attending Middle Georgia State University, when I had a vehicle, I was hired at the District Attorney's Office. The District Attorney told me that he was so impressed with my interview that he was going to find me a ride so I could work at the office. So, I worked in the District Attorney's Office. A month before this happened in November, I became really ill in my body and was attacked after my fast. First, I would just like to say that many people don't understand how hard it is to do college (maintaining honors scholarships), ministry, church duties, and life in general all at the same time as a young person. Because my body had undergone so much stress, it triggered an anxiety attack. I also believe it was demonic/spiritual warfare because of the timing and things that God was doing in my life. Doing ministry, writing books, college, church duties, and life all at once was hard. My heartbeat so hard every day for 11 days. It was so loud that I felt you could hear it across the room. I went to church one night, and a prophet was there. He told my pastor to put oil in me and that the spirit was going to move all over me. He also told me that my car situation was worked out. After the pastor prayed for me, my heart stopped pounding every day.

However, the symptoms were still there, and it started back up. One night when I tried to sleep, I had three panic attacks in a row that was so scary. It was so severe that I literally had to go to work with my mom because I was so afraid and anxious. I remember pacing the floor back and forth. Also, during this whole process, I had been having nightmares the whole time. It was so scary because the devil was telling me he could hurt me and that I should just commit suicide. He told me to stop Millennial For Christ, but I didn't quit. This whole process felt like a NEVER-ENDING NIGHTMARE. It felt like I WAS NOT EVEN in real life. I was in torment, and I was being tortured. I remember in Christmas and New year I isolated myself from my family which was not like me at all because I'm a very outgoing person. I had got to the point where I was scared to be around people, eat, sleep, and get up in the mornings. I was so sad and depressed. I couldn't eat or sleep, and I was always at a high level of unrest. I would have these crying spells all day long. MORNING, EVENING, and NIGHT. I was trying to minister to people not knowing if I was going to make it! I felt so alone and like I was losing my mind! I wouldn't wish this on my worst enemy!

. . .

On December 31st, while at church God told me to read John 4:37-54. In the chapter, he raises a man's son from the dead. He told him at the seventh hour, his son would be alive. Although it didn't look like it when Jesus said it, it was so. Also, there is another story in the Bible where Jesus said a fig tree was dead, but it still looked alive although Christ cursed it. The point is, when God says something, it's done at that moment. This was a very scary experience, but through my faith, quoting the scriptures, rebuking the devil, and having my pastor, my parents, and spiritual brother in Christ pray for me, I was able to overcome the blood of Jesus. Ultimately, I had to decide to be delivered by having faith. This just elevated my faith and took me to another level in God. What the devil meant for evil, God turned it all around for my good! I thank God because statistics show many people who deal with anxiety die or commit suicide. All the Glory goes to God! I know where He has brought me from, and I will never hold back on Him. I lost a lot, but I also gained a lot. I know my journey will not be easy, but God has equipped me mentally, physically, and spiritually for whatever may come my way. These events caused me so much stress, but they made me strong and are helping to push me to my purpose. At different times in my life, I didn't understand why I was bullied, trying to fit in, being sick in my body, wrecking my car, losing family and friends, even experiencing anxiety, but my God had a bigger plan for me, and that was to motivate others. Through everything I went through in high school and college, I kept my head up and I never gave up. When I posted all my achievements, it was to bring glory to God. People probably thought it was an act of arrogance, but I just was so thankful to my God because I know what had to go through to get to that point. I cried every day, I had many sleepless nights, but God was there. He carried me through the storm. I don't know where I would be if God didn't save me.

The Glory After the Story

I want to leave you with two verses. The first verse is Proverbs 3:5-6, and the second verse is Philippians 4:13. My journey has not been perfect, but I had a will, and I never gave up. I owe all my success to my God and family for being a support. I hope it encourages someone. No matter what you face, you can make it! The devil tried everything in his power to stop me. The devil desired to ultimately destroy me. That is his purpose to get you off your assignment and stop you from reaching your destiny. That's what the representation of me being submerged into the tube of deepwater represented. It was not just my grandmother's death, it was all the trials I had to go through. I see the bigger picture. Through everything I went through I came back even stronger. That's what me shooting out the water so fast represented, rivers of living water! The Devil wanted to see me drown, but he did not know that God was my float. God truly had His hands on me, and for that, I am so grateful. God was greater, and He always will be. It doesn't matter how you started or what you have done because you can be redeemed.

PART III

The Guide

The Declaration

YOU! Yes, YOU have the POWER to tell yourself what you can do or have daily! Don't let the enemy tell you otherwise! His assignment is to KILL, STEAL, and DESTROY! Don't let him KILL your JOY! Don't let him steal your PEACE! And Most of all, don't let him DESTROY your SOUL. Speak to EVERY MOUNTAIN in your life with AUTHORITY and say be REMOVED in the name of JESUS! YOU CAN HAVE WHAT YOU SAY! YOU ARE WHAT YOU SAY YOU ARE! I don't know about you, but I am CHILD OF THE HIGHEST! I am of a ROYAL LINEAGE! I DECREE and DECLARE that I will be PROSPEROUS, HEALTHY, and WISE! I am a WINNER because JESUS CHRIST paid it all on the cross! I COMMAND the devil and his little helpers to leave ME, my FAMILY, and EVERYTHING that is CONNECTED to me ALONE! Tell yourself that you have PURPOSE and that you will be everything God has called you to be and, the devil can't defeat you!

Introduction

Dear Kings and Queens,

You are beautiful and handsome inside and out! You do not need a woman or man to validate you. God has so much in store for you. He can open doors and give you platforms you cannot even imagine. You do not have to compete. God has a special section in the kingdom just for you! If you stay in your lane and seek God daily, you will grow and glow. God has so many secrets about you that he wants you to know. Get positioned kings and queens! God can take you further than you can ever imagine. Do you know He desires for us all to prosper? King and queen, do you know you are destined for greatness? Do you know you are from a royal lineage and that you are blessed coming in and going out? Kings and queens, be encouraged because your blessing is on the way! You will walk into your land of milk and honey!

Mikella

PS: I have listed verses from various scriptures, and I have a song for each day that serves as a reference of inspiration for you to listen to as you read these chapters. I do not own copyrights to any of these songs. You will need a journal and pen when completing the guide because I have also included quotes and activities with each day to help inspire you.

Day 1
ALWAYS MAKE TIME FOR GOD

Song: **"Make Room"** by Jonathan McReynolds

Quote: Do not forget to commune with God! Do not just come to him when you need him!

Dear Purposed One,

You can never spend too much time with God, but you can spend too little. In your daily life, you can become so busy with work, school, etc. and let the cares of this world overwhelm you when you should be humbly seeking God's face. I learned to acknowledge the Holy Spirit every morning when I wake up. I say, "Holy Spirit, what is God's will for me today? How can I be a blessing and a witness to someone? Order my footsteps." You can't expect your life to be peaceful if you are not even trying to communicate with God. I remember a time when I needed direction on how to do a project. When I prayed, the information that I needed was downloaded into me instantly. I was able to present the information to my peers immediately. I remember a time when a person I knew needed me to be witness to them about the Lord. God woke me out of my sleep and told me to minister to them. The shackles were broken, and God received all the glory! Hallelujah! God is the ultimate peacemaker and everything else you need. His mercies are new every morning. **You cannot make it in these difficult times without pressing into His presence.** You are not designed to run this race on your own, so stop trying to do it alone. **You must make it into His presence and seek Him daily to maintain and improve your walk with God**.

IT'S IN THE WORD

But seek ye first the kingdom of God, and his righteousness; and all these things shall be added unto you.
Matthew 6:33 KJV

But thou, when thou prayest, enter into thy closet, and when thou hast shut thy door, pray to thy Father which is in secret; and thy Father which seeth in secret shall reward thee openly.
Matthew 6:6 KJV

Study to shew thyself approved unto God, a workman that needeth not to be ashamed, rightly dividing the word of truth.
2 Timothy 2:15 KJV

~

Journal/Activity Time

God wants to be included in every part of your life, even the parts that seem insignificant. He wants to be with you when you go out to eat, for a walk, and even while you are driving alone.

I challenge you to spend time with God daily whether it be through fasting, praying, going to church, reading the Bible, or simply talking to him. Increase your time with God weekly. You can add on 10 minutes or even an hour. Just make sure you press into the secret place.

Day 2
BE HUMBLE

Song: **"Gracefully Broken"** by Tasha Cobbs

Quote: All is well let God be your helper!

Dear Purposed One,

Please be humble because doing so will take you very far in life. I remember I was 19, when I had my first free vehicle. I had just obtained my Associate degree, received many high accolades, was hired at the district attorney's Office, and was heading into my junior year of college. I had it going on, and I became very proud. I had my independence. I did not want to listen to anyone and did my own thing. One week in July, I went on vacation, and my parents told me not to drive on a particular highway. Guess what? I did it anyway. The first time everything went just fine. I tried it again, and **I heard a still voice telling me not to go in that direction, but I went anyway. Boom!** I ran into another vehicle, and I almost lost my life. Now I must insert this in sadly – I disobeyed God twice. This is going to sound funny, but I was most definitely wrong for what I did. I ran into a ditch on June 1, 2018, by backing out of a yard. I had my friend in the car with me, and she had no idea that I was not supposed to be allowing others to get in my vehicle.

I never told my parents about it until sometime after I wrecked my car. Now the vehicle I received as a gift is totaled, and I had only had it for three months. I wondered if I would still be able to work at the district attorney's office, but God worked it out. I felt like Yolanda Adams in her song, ***I'm Gonna Be Ready***. She said, "I was free to do what I wanted to. Lost everything, but I still had You. You showed me your grace. Now my life's renewed and I thank You. In another part of the song, she said, "Lord, don't let me make the same mistakes over and over again."

You can have it all, and God can take it right in an instance. Also, be humble and likable. Never get to the point where you think you are better than someone else. Sometimes the people who can help you get to the next level in your life or purpose will not look important. You may never know who you are in the presence of and who God has sent to bless your life. During my humbling season, I sat at home, and I just went to school online. It was a big transition because I was used to being involved, being recognized, and doing great things! I felt like a "nobody" at this point because I lost everything that made me feel like a "somebody". When all along, I was a nobody who had power through an almighty God! I had to realize that there was a new season in my life and that I needed to humble myself, worship, surrender, and shift with God. God also revealed to me that my humble season was preparing me for my future. He needed me to sit down so He could show me the wonderful plan that He had for my life and prepare me for it. God gracefully broke me for greatness!

Focus on God even more on the mountain top! That is how you will receive the overflow by acknowledging that He is the reason why you are there. Please remain humble because it can **cost you the very thing you value**.

After going through a year of humbling, I went through a year and a half of blessings! I was blessed to start my ministry and raise 5,000 dollars to go to South Africa. I graduated early without debt, and I completed my first photoshoot. I even gained all of my weight back that I had lost due to anxiety, and I was in the Word Network magazine. God continues to amaze me!

IT'S IN THE WORD

He guides the humble in what is right and teaches them his way.
Psalms 25:9

Before a downfall the heart is haughty, but humility comes before honor.
Proverbs 18:12

Humble yourselves before the Lord, and he will lift you up.
James 4:10

In the same way, you who are younger, submit yourselves to your elders. All of you, clothe yourselves with humility toward one another, because, "God opposes the proud but shows favor to the humble."
1 Peter 5:5

Journal/Activity Time

I challenge you to think about everything you are trying to do on your own and release it to God. At the beginning of each sentence, you write I RELEASE. Then speak and write I trust you God over and over. It's something about writing and speaking a thing that brings about relief. Believe it, Write it, Receive it.

Example
I RELEASE trying to get into my dream college to you Lord.

Day 3
PATIENCE

Song: **"I Don't Mind Waiting"** by Juanita Bynum

Quote: Please be at peace, God is turning your situation all the way around!

Dear Purposed One,

Please be patient. In the Bible, patience is listed as a fruit of the spirit and it is very important. It's very imperative for the Christian walk. God does not withhold any good thing from us for His pleasure or out of being mean. Also, it is not that He does not desire for us to have what we want. God wants what is best for His children. There was a time I would cry almost every Sunday. I would be high in church and then come home and cry because I was so tired, and honestly, I felt like things were not happening fast enough. I had to be patient to make it through college; it just seemed like such a long process. I had to be patient and wait for my Internship (to come back around) after declining it the first time. I also had to be patient to get a job I applied for seven months in advance. I had to have the patience to maintain it because it was not an easy job to get. God blessed me with a free car because I waited. I almost stepped out His will and bought a vehicle, but He told me to wait, so I did just that. God just wanted me to stop complaining and just trust Him.

Oftentimes, He holds things from us because we are not ready or because the very thing we may desire could destroy us. For example, newborn babies cannot eat solid food because they don't have teeth. Many times, Christians want to eat solid foods and they are only newborns; if God gave them the solid food they would choke and die. You can't rush God because He sees from the womb to the tomb. In Jeremiah 1:5, He says, "I knew you before I formed you in your mother's womb." Why is it so hard to trust a God who created us and knows everything about us? Sadly, if God gave you everything you wanted, more than likely you would stop praising Him because you would feel you have no need for Him.

In my opinion, when you feel you have no need for God, that turns into a proud spirit. When you get things ahead of time they can make you proud. Before God blesses you, He has to kill things in us that are not of Him. When He kills things in you, He knows that He can trust you with materialistic gifts. The thing is, you must first be willing to let Him remove the toxic things within you.

Pray in God's will because you may be praying for something that is not beneficial to you. Sometimes God will give you something you asked for just to prove a point to you. Because you were impatient, He may allow that thing to be given to you, but it will cause you much heartache, grief, and even embarrassment. We could also destroy something we are not ready for. Most of the great things that happened in my life were unexpected. It's when I tried to force things and put me first, instead of God, that I messed up.

When you stop trying to make a thing happen, then God can do His best work. God knows all your heart desires, but He's not moved by complaining and you stepping in His way. God changes His time for no one! Every perfect gift comes from the Father. Go with the flow! God has a time and season for everything and all gifts are beautiful in His timing.

IT'S IN THE WORD

To every thing there is a season, and a time to every purpose under the heaven. He hath made every thing beautiful in his time: also he hath set the world in their heart, so that no man can find out the work that God maketh from the beginning to the end.
Ecclesiastes 3:1,11

Rest in the LORD and wait patiently for Him; Do not fret because of him who prospers in his way, because of the man who carries out wicked schemes.
Psalm 37:7

Knowing that the testing of your faith produces endurance.
Consider it all joy, my brethren, when you encounter various
trials, and let endurance have its perfect result, so that you may
be perfect and complete, lacking in nothing.

James 1:2-4

Journal/Activity Time

I challenge you to speak this in prayer and in the atmosphere all
day. When you speak you cause an automatic shift.

Day 4
RUN TO GOD

Song: **"Run to the Father"** by Cody Carnes

Quote: Everything you need is in the word of God!

Dear Purposed One,

God is all that you need. He cares for you even though your circumstances may not show it. There was a time in my life when I was depressed because my grandmother died. I had lost my best friend; the one who understood me was gone forever! To continue, I did not get a scholarship to the school I desired to go to, I got into a wreck, went through depression, and more heartbreaks. I felt like I did not have one friend to talk to about my situation. I was holding all this pain inside. I was going to church every Sunday crying out as hard as I could to get a breakthrough. However, Sunday after Sunday, still nothing. I had never experienced such pain in my life. It is like everything was bubbling inside of me all at once. I did not have anyone to talk to, and I was *so tired*. I did not know what to do and I ran to everything…but God. I tried going to the club, eating, drinking, dating, shopping, etc. I am here to tell you none of those materialistic things filled me like Jesus. None of those things could fill the "huge God voids" in my life. Only getting closer in my relationship with Him could.

I had to examine myself because I was ministering to people and telling them to do one thing, and I was not even doing it. Once the storm hit me, it hit very hard. It was sad that **I was helping get others to get a breakthrough,** and I could **not even get a breakthrough myself**. I had a word for everyone, but no one knew how depressed I was.

You can *try* to fill voids with materialistic things all day long, but nothing can bring peace and satisfaction as Jesus can! I kicked a long time, and I still kick against the prick every now and then, but I am trying to be obedient and give God a "yes" now. When you know He has called you to do something, just give Him a "yes" and He will do the rest. **Stop kicking** and just say, "Okay Lord." I got *tired*, so I was like, "You know what – **I'm going try it Your way, Lord**." When you **align your plans with God's plans,** He will walk you into your destiny. When you run to everything but God, it will leave you feeling guilt and shame on top of the mess you already have made.

I am free, and the joy God has given me is unexplainable. God loves you, and there is a purpose for everything you go through. Sometimes, he will allow us to go through things to show us **we cannot make it without Him** and to build our faith. Also, the things we go through *are not always for ourselves*. We go through tests and trials, so His power can be manifested, and He can get the glory. I was a broken mess, but God gave me a reason to keep believing. God gave me a purpose to keep on breathing. Face your pain and run to God - He won't fail you.

IT'S IN THE WORD

I run to you God; I run for dear life.
Psalm 31:1, MSG

Be good to me, God — and now! I've run to you for dear life. I'm hiding out under your wings until the hurricane blows over. I call out to High God, the God who holds me together. He sends orders from heaven and saves me, he humiliates those who kick me around. God delivers generous love, he makes good on his word.
Psalm 57:1-3, MSG

I have fought the good fight, I have finished the race, I have kept the faith. Now there is in store for me the crown of righteousness, which the Lord, the righteous Judge, will award to me on that day – and not only to me, but also to all who have longed for his appearing" word."
2 Timothy 4:7-8

Do not worry about your physical well-being. People who don't know any better run after all the things they want, but your Heavenly Father knows your needs. Run for his kingdom and his righteousness then everything that you need will be taken care of.

Matthew 6:32-33, *paraphrased*

I will lift up mine eyes unto the hills, from whence cometh my help. 2 My help cometh from the Lord, which made heaven and earth.

Psalm 121: 1-2

Journal/Activity Time

I challenge you to read a verse that you have never read. Also, I challenge you to find a verse concerning your particular situation.

Example
Identify the Particular Situation - My boyfriend/girlfriend broke my heart.
Research
Google Search : Where in the Bible can I find a scripture on God healing a person of heartbreak?
Solution
The Lord is close to the brokenhearted and saves those who are crushed in spirit (Psalm 34:18)

Day 5
FOCUS

Song: **"Worth Fighting For"** by Brian Courtney Wilson

Quote: Focus your attention to God and everything will fall into place!

Dear Purposed One,

Now that you have run to God, you must keep your focus. In your pursuit of living for God and figuring out your purpose, you will come across many obstacles and distractions. I had to focus to earn a bachelor's degree early. I went to school full-time three semesters straight while doing ministry, and I encountered many distractions. These distractions included failing tests and having to bring my grades to A averages before the end of the semester, feeling drained, dealing with grief, etc. During this time, my faith was really tested. I overcame these obstacles in my life because I put my focus on God. I would always **listen to worship music, praise God, and pray**

throughout the day. I would also pick out a verse from scripture to read and meditate on it. Because my focus was so on God and what He wanted me to do, **I had little time to concentrate on negative things** or my grandmother's death. I love the song that my father taught me. In the song it says, "so forget about yourself, concentrate on Him, and worship Him." Worship is a great way to focus on God. When you worship, you're dying to the flesh, and you do not have any time to think about the cares of this world – there's only time to focus on Jesus. When Job (one of the wealthiest men in the Bible) lost everything he owned, he humbled himself and worshipped God. You have to have the mindset that no matter what, God is still God. If you lose everything, you'll never lose God because He is eternal.

IT'S IN THE WORD

And said, "Naked came I out of my mother's womb, and naked shall I return thither: the LORD gave, and the LORD hath taken away; blessed be the name of the LORD."
Job 1:21 King James Version (KJV)

∾

Let your eyes look directly forward, and your gaze be straight before you.
Proverbs 4:25

∾

I can do all things through him who strengthens me.
Philippians 4:13

I will meditate on your precepts and fix my eyes on your ways.
Psalm 119:15

Set your minds on things that are above, not on things that are on earth.
Colossians 3:2

Finally, brethren, whatsoever things are true, whatsoever things are honest, whatsoever things are just, whatsoever things are pure, whatsoever things are lovely, whatsoever things are of good report; if there be any virtue, and if there be any praise, think on these things.
Philippians 4:8

Journal/Activity Time

I challenge you to take a few deep breaths. Inhale. Exhale! I want you to journal ways you can focus and reach your goals. Also, make a vision board after writing your goals. You can hang this board in your room, or anywhere you want as a reminder to strive for success daily.

Example
Identify Your Goal/Goals
I would like to become a better cook.
One Way To Focus
I could make time in my schedule to watch the Cooking channel every day for 30 minutes.

Day 6
BE PRODUCTIVE

Song: **"Go Get It"** by Mary Mary

Quote: God has something special for me (Repeat this quote)!

Dear Purposed One,

There is so much you can contribute to the kingdom. God has something unique for you. Napoleon Hill once said, **"Time is valuable, and when it is gone, it is gone. Time is wealth, and unlike money, when it is gone, you cannot replace it".** Therefore, you should seek God daily by asking, "How can I be productive?"

Let me be very transparent about my sad truth. When I was 18, I received the word that I was going to marry a man that was going to be a provider. I somewhat went into an unproductive state of mind after that, primarily because I was dating a guy in the military. My thoughts were I was going to marry, be cute, and not have to do anything. Then God dealt with me; He said, "No man wants a lazy woman, whether she has to work or not. The man I am calling you to be with will do a lot of work in ministry, so you need to get on the ball right now. I have work for you to do right now in your single season; as a matter of fact, I'm not going to release you until you get to it."

Catch what I'm about to say – this is not just for the women. Some Godly men are seeking a wife, and you need to be working not only for the natural but the kingdom as well. You cannot have it together in one area and lack in the other. Furthermore, a prophet can misunderstand God sometimes, and I may not even marry that man. We all have a responsibility and a unique audience. For me, God told me my assignment was to start my organization, Millennial for Christ, and to write this book.

God may assign you to go to the hospital and pray for the patients, preach, social media ministry, etc. You have to seek God, as I did, and He will show you. Jesus was about his Father's business and obeyed everything God told him to do. Because of this, He completed all His assignments in a short period – three years. If you obey God when He's telling you to, you can receive all He has for you in a short period, if that's His will.

God does not have favorites, so no deed is too big or small in His eyes. Don't let resources limit you. I had an iPhone 5 when I started Millennial for Christ and my YouTube channel in 2018. I posted a Monday motivational video every week, and I've never missed one in two years. I literally had to delete ALL my apps and other things off my phone to make space every week to create my video. I would even have to edit my videos for hours. I wanted to quit many times, but I just couldn't because I knew I was in the will of God. In my last year of college, my advisor told me that I could graduate soon if I took classes full-time the entire year. After praying, I decided to take the classes. I never even thought that I could graduate early until my last year of college. After working many hours on videos, I couldn't quit, and now I have reached 12,000 people. I'm an international speaker with an international ministry (South Africa), and I have impacted almost 30 nations through my blog and ministry. Know that when you are faithful over the small, He will make you a ruler over many. That is biblical. He wants you to seek him and obey him once he gives you an assignment. That is how you can be productive for the kingdom. **Be a go-getter for Jesus**!

IT'S IN THE WORD

Whatever you do, work heartily, as for the Lord and not for men, knowing that from the Lord you will receive the inheritance as your reward. You are serving the Lord Christ.
Colossians 3:23-24

For we are God's handiwork, created in Christ Jesus to do good works, which God prepared in advance for us to do.
Ephesians 2:10

～

And He said to them, "Why did you seek Me? Did you not know
that I must be about My Father's business?"
Luke 2:49

～

And God blessed them, and God said unto them, Be fruitful, and
multiply, and replenish the earth, and subdue it: and have
dominion over the fish of the sea, and over the fowl of the air,
and over every living thing that moveth upon the earth.
Genesis 1:28

～

Four things on earth are small, but they are exceedingly wise: the
ants are a people not strong, yet they provide their food in the
summer; the rock badgers are a people not mighty, yet they make
their homes in the cliffs; the locusts have no king, yet all of them
march in rank; the lizard you can take in your hands, yet it is in
kings' palaces.
Prov. 30:24-26

～

The hand of the diligent will rule, while the slothful will be put to
forced labor.
Prov. 12:24

～

Do you see a man skillful in his work? He will stand before kings; he will not stand before obscure men.

Prov. 22:29

~

Journal/Activity Time

I challenge you to repeat this quote today! Write it on a sticky note, and post it on your wall!

Day 7
PUT IN THE WORK

Song: **"Yes"** by Shekinah Glory Ministry

Quote: Hard work always pays off!

Dear Purposed One,

God did not create you to be lazy. Anything in life worth having or of value will not be easy to obtain. When I was a leader in JROTC, my sergeant instilled this quote in me – "If it were easy then anyone would do it". God created the man to work and be a provider. God created the woman to tend to her household and be a businesswoman. Yes, women, you are supposed to work too; stop waiting for a man to take care of you.

The spiritual realm works just like the natural realm. What you put in is what you will get out. God is not going to place anything in your lap. In the Bible, it says those who thirst and hunger after righteousness shall be filled. In James 2:17 it says, "Thus also faith by itself, if it does not have works, is dead." If you're thirsty and hungry for God, you are producing because you will repeatedly feed yourself with the word, pray, fast, and worship God. In the Bible, God commands us to work while it is day. Sometimes you will have to pray for a long time. Sometimes you will have to fast and read the word all day.

Many saints believe they can receive spiritual power, but they are not sacrificing or putting in work. In ministry, you will not always have time to eat, sleep, or do fun things. However, it does not give you a right to be lazy. Seeking God every day is a strategic way for you as a believer to get spiritual information and education directly from heaven to increase your faith. God says He will renew your strength and that you will reap a harvest if you faint not (See Isaiah 40:31, Galatians 6:9). Most of the time, when people are lazy, they quit at everything. You have to discipline your flesh because laziness can take it over. What if I would have given up in high school because I failed a class? What if I would have stopped when I wanted to in JROTC? What if I would have quit when things got hard in college? I'll tell you what – I'd never graduated with honors, never known my full potential, or received many awards, and I'd never have received my degrees. God gives us words about our future, but there's always something required, and if you are too lazy, your prophetic words will never come to pass. I didn't just write this book, but I worked to pay for the publishing of this book. In other words, when God gives you an assignment he doesn't just place in your lap. If you want all that God has for you, get out and work! Hard work always pays off in the end.

. . .

I'm just an example, and I am here to encourage you that God has a great plan for you (Jeremiah 29:11). Like my favorite artist, Jonathan McReynolds, says in his new single Try, "I gotta make a sincere effort to be all that you called me to be, God! I just don't want to stay here living beneath! I owe it to me to at least try! Tell me what I need to do so I can be close to you! I only want to make you smile! This time is different! Tell heaven to watch me while I try!"

IT'S IN THE WORD

Blessed are those who hunger and thirst for righteousness, for they shall be filled.
Matthew 5:6

∽

For as the body **without** the spirit is **dead**, so **faith without works is dead** also.
James 2:26

∽

Enter into his gates with thanksgiving, and into his courts with praise: be thankful unto him, and bless his name.
Psalm 100:4

∽

Diligent hands will rule, but laziness ends in forced labor.
Proverbs 12:24

~

A sluggard's appetite is never filled, but the desires of the diligent are fully satisfied.

Proverbs 13:4

~

Journal/Activity Time

I challenge you to find new ways to do a better job in all your life activities.

Example

Identify what you are good at: Witnessing to people

A Way I Can Do This Better

I can read my Bible five more minutes a day. Instead of my goal being to minister to 2 people a week I'm going to try to boost it to three.

Day 8
ACCEPTANCE

Song: **"Adopted"** by Casey J

Quote: I am what God says I am! (Repeat this quote)

Dear Purposed One,

The world, not God, puts all this pressure on us to be this and that, to have your dream career, be successful and married at a certain age. You may be feeling pressure to look a specific way, drive a nice car, or have a big house. The truth is none of those things truly validate you. **What does God say?** God says that you **are fearfully and wonderfully made**. In high school, I was bullied so badly that it affected me even in college. I had low self-esteem and constantly felt I had to prove myself. Now I can look at and wear my natural hair and it doesn't bother me to do so. I still wear weave, yes, but now it's different; it's not because I'm ashamed, but I wear it now just because I like it and it is convenient. During my high school years, I saw so many girls who had low self-esteem because they didn't like their shapes, hair, face, and were teased often by other teens. Any time I see a girl who feels low because of what others are saying, I give them an encouraging word. I say things like, "You have to love yourself first, and what others think won't matter. Embrace your flaws because no one is perfect. Remember not to be jealous of the next female, but compliment her." The most important thing I tell them, in my opinion, is that Jesus loves you, and as long as you have His approval what others think is irrelevant.

Many of my relationships could not work because I wanted affirmation from guys. For a long time, I looked for my worth in a guy. I didn't believe someone could really love me for me. The feelings of being inadequate made me very prideful. I was pretty all along, but once people started telling me all the time, it went to my head. Not only that, but I achieved a lot of things and let that go to my head.

One day I realized that I was not free from what happened to me in high school, and I had to put how I felt on the altar. **I needed to get my value from God, and so should you. I had to deal with the issue before the issue dealt with me**. Growing up, I was always told that I was special and cannot be like everybody else. You should accept that you are precious and uniquely designed by God because it is an honor. You may not be perfect, but you are **still God's masterpiece,** and He loves you **just the way you are**.

IT'S IN THE WORD

Here is a trustworthy saying that deserves full acceptance: Christ
Jesus came into the world to save sinners—of whom I am the
worst.
1 Timothy 1:15

∾

I praise you because I am fearfully and wonderfully made; your
works are wonderful, I know that full well.
Psalm 139:14

∾

All those the Father gives me will come to me, and whoever
comes to me I will never drive away.
John 6:37

∾

I say then, God has not rejected His people, has He? May it
never be! For I too am an Israelite, a descendant of Abraham, of
the tribe of Benjamin.
Romans 11:1

∾

Journal/Activity Time

I challenge you to repeat this quote today! Write it on a sticky
note, and post it on your wall!

Day 9
PEER PRESSURE OR JUST PRESSURE?

Song: **"Pressure"** by Jonathan McReynolds

Quote: Your validation comes from Christ!

Dear Purposed One,

Now that you know you are accepted, please don't fall into peer pressure. Peer pressure is dangerous because some habits you fall into will be hard to break, and they can affect your life now and later. My issue used to be trying to fit in high school. I was bullied – I mean *really* bullied. I was talked about because my parents were ministers, and I lived a very sheltered lifestyle. I was picked at because I was a nerd. My eyes are big, but they really stood out when I was younger. My peers used to call me Eyekella. I used to have a lot of hair, and a lot of it came out, and until this day, I still do not know why (I assume it was a bad perm). I am pretty sure you can figure that I was picked on because of that as well; it used to hurt my feelings so much. My peers also talked about the way I dressed and styled my hair. I finally attempted to prevent being bullied by hanging with the wrong people and doing things I shouldn't have done. I was not allowed to have a phone, so I would use my tablet as a phone because my parents did not know that I could do that. Lol! Also, my so-called friends (because they weren't real ones) would sneak me phones to school. My mom blocked me from the Wi-Fi at our house once she realized I was using my tablet as a phone, so I would sneak and use the neighbor's Wi-Fi. WOW! I would try to dress and wear my hair like all the other girls. Once I started doing this, then I began to pick on people (I didn't feel good about myself, so I was trying to take the attention off myself. I didn't do this for long). I remember one day, I had on one outfit when I left home, and I changed once I made it to school. Guess what – I got caught. The principal called my mom, and I had to leave school. One day in gym class, I drank some alcohol, and thank God I didn't get drunk because I was way underage. I am intelligent, but in my ninth-grade year, I failed a math class because I was trying to fit in. I would walk into the classroom, go off on the teacher, and then go to sleep. I failed a class for the first and only time. I realized I didn't know who I was. I had to find my identity in Christ. When you know who you are in Christ, you will not succumb to peer pressure. After that, I never let anyone, or anything, get me off track from my academics. I had to make 100's in a lot of my classes, but I eventually graduated from high school *with honors*. My principal and others who knew I failed a class were so amazed. My mother still works for the school system, and some of my classmates come up there. She tells me my classmates/school administrators look up to me to this day for being different and that I'm doing good with my life. They desire to be like me. To God be the glory!

. . .

IT'S IN THE WORD

You shall not follow the masses in doing evil, nor shall you testify
in a dispute so as to turn aside after a multitude in order to
pervert justice;
Exodus 23:2

∾

A man of too many friends comes to ruin, but there is a friend
who sticks closer than a brother.
Proverbs 18:24

∾

He who walks with wise men will be wise, but the companion of
fools will suffer harm.
Proverbs 13:20

∾

And do not be conformed to this world, but be transformed by
the renewing of your mind, so that you may prove what the will
of God is, that which is good and acceptable and perfect will
suffer harm.
Romans 12:2

∾

No temptation has overtaken you that is not common to man.
God is faithful, and he will not let you be tempted beyond your

ability, but with the temptation he will also provide the way of
escape, that you may be able to endure it.

1 Corinthians 10:13

Journal/Activity Time

When you feel pressured, I challenge you to accept your process.
If you know that your worth is truly in Christ and that he has a
great plan for you, you will realize that the pressure people or
even you put on yourself will go away. Remember that whatever
God allows, he can change.

Day 10
BAD COMPANY CORRUPTS GOOD MANNERS

Song: **"Maintain"** by Jonathan McReynolds

Quote: God if it interferes with my relationship then I do not want it.

Dear Purposed One,

You cannot mix and mingle with just anyone when you are anointed and have a calling from God. Also, everyone does not have your best interests at heart. When choosing your friends, **examine the fruits they are producing to see if they are of the spirit** and ask God for a spirit of **discernment**. They may be trying to set you up. The Bible tells us to keep on the full armor because surely the devil is seeking whom he may devour. In my first year of college, I backslid because I got hooked up with some of the wrong people. I went to the club a few times. That was so out of my character for a girl who has been in church for her whole life. I thank God for His grace because out of the three times I went to the club, there was a shooting one time right after I left. I could have been shot at and killed! You may not believe this, but eventually, if you surround yourself with people who have bad habits, you will obtain bad habits as well. I have one friend who always encourages me to do right. My friend holds me accountable and keeps me in the will of God any time I feel that I'm going to do wrong. This relationship has elevated me mentally, physically, and spiritually. Good friends push you forward in every area of your life, and the bad company holds you back. It is vital to hang around like-minded people because they will encourage you to be your best self. You can die from making the wrong decisions. If you surround yourself with people who have good habits, you will have good habits. Satan wants to taint your testimony. The people you hang with **will affect your destiny**. Be around people **who are like-minded and trying to pursue Christ with you**. Associate yourself with people in ministry that are where you want to be. There is nothing wrong with having a role model. I desire to be a role model for my generation. I want people to experience God the way I have.

IT'S IN THE WORD

Be ye not unequally yoked together with unbelievers: for what fellowship hath righteousness with unrighteousness? and what communion hath light with darkness?
2 Corinthians 6:14-17

Do not be misled: "Bad company corrupts good character."

1 Corinthians 15:33 NIV

Dear friends, do not believe every spirit, but test the spirits to see whether they are from God, because many false prophets have gone out into the world.
1 John 4:1

And if your right hand causes you to stumble, cut it off and throw it away. It is better for you to lose one part of your body than for your whole body to go into hell.
Matthew 5:30

Journal/Activity Time

I challenge you to write down your friends/connections. Then ask God who should and shouldn't be in your life. For each person who gets to stay, ask what role does this particular person play in my life. Ask him if this is a permanent person or a seasonal person.

Day 11
FEAR

Song: **"Fearless"** by Jasmine Murray

Quote: You should be willing to be uncomfortable for Jesus!

Dear Purposed One,

Take the limits off God! You never know what you can do until you try. Fear is a **hindrance and a paralyzer**. Whatever makes you the most nervous is what you should work on because more than likely it is attached to your purpose. If you truly love God, your love for Him will cast out all fear! Sometimes things seem greater than you, but if God has brought you to something, He will bring you through it. Check out David and Goliath in the Bible. Goliath was a giant, and David was small in stature. Yet, David knocked Goliath out with a stone and then used the giant's sword to cut off the giant's head! In David's human strength he could not defeat Goliath, but in God's strength, we can do all things. Step out of fear even if that mountain seems high; when you take that step of faith, God will fight for you.

When I was going through a spiritual warfare and dealing with anxiety, I was very scared at first. The reason I was able to overcome this fear is, because I kept quoting the verse that God has not given me the spirit of fear (2 Timothy 1:7).

I've always feared public speaking, believe it or not. In 2019, I was very reluctant about going to South Africa once I found out that I had to speak. I thought it was just a vacation when I first applied. Through much prayer and fasting, I killed my flesh in of this situation. I also practiced by speaking to the youth at my church every Monday night before leaving. I was taught in a business class that you are less likely to be afraid if you are knowledgeable and prepared for your presentation. Faith without works is dead; study (prepare) to show yourself approved (see James 2:14-26, 2 Timothy 2:15 for exact scripture). Fear is in the flesh. If you walk with God in the Spirit, He gives you the grace to carry out His will. You can't walk in purpose in the flesh; it just won't work because the flesh wants what the flesh wants.

Fear is preventing a lot of people from reaching their full potential, but you can overcome it. Sometimes, you feel like you are not able to do something when you really are. Sometimes people feel like they are not smart enough. There will always be someone better at doing something and smarter than you, but you can't be afraid. You may even feel they are not physically capable. The only way it can be overcome is by committed practice, study, and a willingness to go through with it.

. . .

There was a determined man named Michael Jordan. He tried out for a basketball team, and he didn't make the cut the first time. He never gave fear a chance to set in, and he never gave up. He didn't become dismayed; he just kept practicing and bettering himself. Eventually, he became arguably one of the best basketball players in the world. It's scary trying to do something you failed at before, but you have to do it to get over that fear.

Fear is not easy for anyone to handle, but it can be defeated. The more you do something, the more comfortable it becomes. The more adjusted you become, the less nervous you will be. You have to be determined, prepared, and willing to face your giant. No matter how nervous you are, you have to push yourself and just do it. Put your best effort forth, and if it doesn't work out don't let fear stop you from trying again.

IT'S IN THE WORD

David and Goliath – 1 Samuel, Chapter 17

The LORD is with me; I will not be afraid. What can mere mortals do to me?
Psalm 118:6

For God hath not given us the spirit of fear; but of power, and of love, and of a sound mind.

2 Timothy 1:7 KJV

There is no fear in love, but perfect love casts out fear. For fear has to do with punishment, and whoever fears has not been perfected in love.

John 4:18

Journal/Activity Time

I challenge you to go after that thing that scares you! Practice and step out! You have to conquer it head on! Always remember that If God is calling you to something he is with you. He is greater than anything that will come against you.

Example
Fear: Speaking in class
Solution
Be the first to volunteer to speak in class the next time the opportunity comes.

Day 12
DIE TO SELF

Song: **"Purpose Over Pleasure"** by Jonathan Traylor

Quote: When you really love God, living for him is a sacrifice, but his grace is sufficient.

Purposed One,

Dying to your flesh is a tough one – well at least it was for me. Killing your flesh is never easy, but you cannot walk in the will of God fully unless you do so. The Bible says that the spirit is willing, but the flesh is weak. You must be very disciplined to walk in the Holy Spirit. When you are dying to self, you are pushing your desires back and bringing God's will to the forefront so that God's will can happen. In the Bible, it says that some things only come by fasting and praying (Matthew 17:21). I realized the best strategies for dying to self are prayer and fasting.

Pray, fast, and travail until you feel something inside of you break. For me, public speaking and singing were some of my issues. I did not sing or speak in public to my full potential because of fear. When you walk in fear, that is not of the spirit of God. I was consumed by what man thought about me rather than God's opinion of me. I had to read verses about fear over and over again until it became a part of my spirit, and I was no longer afraid.

Throughout the past few years, God gave me strategic techniques and sacrifices to prosper over my flesh. When I had unGodly friendships and relationships, I had to Block, Scroll, and Delete them off social media and completely out of my life. Instead of going through old habits and cycles, I had to stop making the same mistakes over and over again by disciplining the mind. I believed that I could make the right choices, and I avoided situations that could be compromising. I had to sacrifice money by sowing seeds even when my bank account may not have looked like I could do so. I had to make changes in the way I talked (if you say inappropriate things stop it), and acted (act professionally, thinking before you speak). I stopped doing old things and hanging in unhealthy environments.

I changed by spending more time with God (talking to God, praying, reading the word, going to church even more, putting my phone down, and ministering to others even when I wanted to be doing something else. Sometimes, you have to lose sleep due to God waking you up to pray, due to preparing for a word, due to doing whatever God is instructing you to do!

I spent much time alone because it is in isolation periods that God does his most powerful downloading into our mind and spirit. When I spent time alone, I tapped into my gifts and talents that included singing, speaking, missionary, and outreach work, etc. When I was alone, I fasted because sometimes, to hear God and be purified, you have to push the plate back. I also praised my way through because no matter what circumstance you find yourself in! Worship is a lifestyle!

My ministry has reached many, and they have received breakthroughs. The favor, accomplishments, and blessings of God are in my life at 22 years old because I sacrifice for God. People always tell me you are so favored and blessed, but they don't see behind the scenes. Everything I have is not because I'm just entitled to it or even always deserve it. However, I do sacrifice what I can unto God, and I have parents who offer a sacrifice to God and stand in the gap in prayer on my behalf as well.

God is calling for thirsty and hungry people in this season! I would never tell you all something I don't do myself. I'm not bragging, but I do all these things. If you want to favor and anointing on your life, you have to sacrifice. There is no other way around it. You have to be uncomfortable. You do things you don't necessarily enjoy. You do all this, keeping in mind that the glory will go to God! You and God know what you need to sacrifice! When you make that spiritual offering, watch how the blessings will flow! Watch God!

IT'S IN THE WORD

I beseech you therefore, brethren, by the mercies of God, that ye present your bodies a living sacrifice, holy, acceptable unto God, which is your reasonable service. And be not conformed to this world: but be ye transformed by the renewing of your mind, that ye may prove what is that good, and acceptable, and perfect, will of God.

Romans 12:1-2

And put on the new self, which in the likeness of God has been created in righteousness and holiness of the truth.

Ephesians 4:24

∿

So as to live the rest of the time in the flesh no longer for the lusts of men, but for the will of God.

1 Peter 4:2

∿

He must increase, but I must decrease.

John 3:30

∿

I have been crucified with Christ; and it is no longer I who live, but Christ lives in me; and the life which I now live in the flesh I live by faith in the Son of God, who loved me and gave Himself up for me.

Galatians 2:20

∿

Journal/Activity Time

I challenge you to remind yourself that Jesus died for you. If you have a cross necklace, or any apparel or accessories wear it today. I actually have a necklace I wear everyday from South Africa that means persistence. It reminds me daily to persevere in my pursuit of Christ and my purpose.

Day 13
PRAYER

Song: **"Pray"** by CeCe Winans

Quote: Pray always for guidance, protection, and blessings.

Dear Purposed One,

Prayer is so vital in your walk with God. You need to pray before you make any decision, whether it is a small one or a major one. It is *just that serious.*

I remember praying before going to South Africa. I had seen a confirmation post the morning of the day I found out I won the scholarship to Africa. The post said, you are being put on the mind of someone who can help you this month. This was also confirmation to a prophecy I received in April of 2019. The prophet told me after the month of May 2019, I was going to meet a female figure that would help me to get to the next level, and he also said I was called to speak to people all around the world. God gave confirmation through the social media post at 8:46am about the female figure choosing me as the scholarship recipient, and later on that day at 5:21pm.

I had two confirmations, and I was still not fully convinced. I was in the process of 1) deciding if I was going and 2) wondering if I would do a fundraiser so that I could go. I remember that it was on a Saturday that I prayed for confirmation on whether to go and to do the fundraiser. I also prayed for God to give me peace about the situation. That very next day, which was a Sunday, God gave me confirmation and peace through my pastor.

I had people telling me I shouldn't go, I was stressing about deadlines for material, and some days I was straight out scared because it was a new adventure for me (I had never been on a plane or out the country), and I did not know what to expect. However, I knew God was leading me there because I had confirmation through my prayer. When you know God and you know you have heard him don't look at the time or circumstances. God confirmed to me so many times that I was supposed to be in Africa. This one trip has strengthened my faith even the more because everything God said he would do he did it! No matter what opposition I faced, I was determined because I knew that through prayer, my confirmation had come from God. I knew I was in His perfect will for my life at that particular time.

When you pray, you also have to make sure it is in the Spirit so that you are praying the perfect will of God rather than your own. The Bible says, do not lean to your own understanding. The Bible also says, to pray without ceasing. Prayer is also the key to opening the next door in your life. You will not have a relationship with God without communicating with God through prayer. Prayer gives you power! I did not know I could pray until my grandmother was living in her last days. I learned to pray out of desperation of wanting my grandma to live. I remember so vividly telling her to reach and cry out like to God like never before, and I prayed under power like never before. It was magical. I felt like Jeremiah when he said, "it's like fire in my bones"! Prayer gives you the power to fight the enemy, unique power to make miracles happen, and the power to move mountains. Pray when you are doing well or bad, and pray for your future. Prayer gives you the ability to do things you cannot do in your strength. Prayer is your best foundation to stand on.

IT'S IN THE WORD

This is the confidence we have in approaching God: that if we ask anything according to his will, he hears us.

1 John 5:14

If my people, who are called by my name, will humble themselves and pray and seek my face and turn from their wicked ways, then I will hear from heaven, and I will forgive their sin and will heal their land.

2 Chronicles 7:14

Look to the LORD and his strength; seek his face always.
1 Chronicles 16:11

And pray in the Spirit on all occasions with all kinds of prayers and requests. With this in mind, be alert and always keep on praying for all the Lord's people.
Ephesians 6:18

Watch and pray so that you will not fall into temptation. The spirit is willing, but the flesh is weak.
Matthew 26:41

Watch and pray so that you will not fall into temptation. The spirit is willing, but the flesh is weak.

May my prayer be set before you like incense; may the lifting up of my hands be like the evening sacrifice.
Psalm 141:2

Journal/Activity Time

I challenge you to write sticky notes with your prayer requests, and post them on your wall!

Day 14
WORSHIP AND FAVOR

Song: **"More Than Anything"** by Joann Rosario

Quote: God will bless you if you are in position!

Dear Purposed One,

When you are worshipping God and spending much time with Him, worry does not have room to exist. Worshipping God refocuses you. It puts your mind back on God rather than your situation. When you increase your time in worship, God will give you grace and favor just because you are letting him know, "God, I appreciate You and I love You." He loves for us to worship Him even when we have trouble in our life on every side. God acknowledges our drive for Him. True worship is spending time with God daily, pressing your way to church, fasting, and reading your word. Worship is not listening to worship songs; it is a lifestyle. I remember my second year of college, I already had good grades, but some of my professors at school offered me extra credit. Other professors nominated me for awards and paid for my campaign materials when I ran for homecoming queen, but not because of anything I did; it was FAVOR! God blessed me with a free car that others were trying to purchase because of FAVOR! God will have people do things they don't usually do for you because your heart is for HIM. God is a rewarder of those who diligently seek Him. The people who are truly after His heart and seek Him daily will receive favor. Worship God and watch how your life will change.

IT'S IN THE WORD

And without faith it is impossible to please God, because anyone who comes to him must believe that he exists and that he rewards those who earnestly seek him.
Hebrews 11:6

Praising God, and having favour with all the people. And the Lord added to the church daily such as should be saved.
Acts 2:47

Come, let us bow down in worship, let us kneel before the Lord our Maker.
Psalm 95:6

God *is* a Spirit: and they that worship him must worship *him* in spirit and in truth.

John 4:24

∿

Journal/Activity Time

I challenge you to journal new ways you can worship God. Whether it be through singing, praise dancing, or even simply telling him I love you Lord. Make God feel appreciated.

Day 15
PERSEVERING IN THE TEST

Song: **"In the Middle of It"** by Isaac Carree

Quote: You will get tired, but you must see the bigger picture! You are so close, keep pushing!

Dear Purposed One,

In this life, you and your faith will face opposition, tests, and trials, and you will find yourself in unexpected circumstances. Sometimes, you will go through test after test. The worst thing you can do during a test is giving up. During my first two years of college, I would always choose the most challenging professors. When test time came, I would usually fail the first test or two, but with persistence and perseverance, I brought many of my grades from F averages to A averages. Tests will not come to defeat you but to make you stronger. My father wrote a song called Keep Pressing On. In the song, he talks about how Satan will try to tell you that you are not able to do what God has already empowered to do. He believes the way we should handle Satan is by telling him that God is enabling us to keep pressing (See 1 John 4:4, Philippians 3:14, and Philippians 4:13). Usually, when trials intensify, that is when you are on the edge of a breakthrough. What to do in the test? Don't give up! If you keep pushing and fighting, you will conquer the enemy.

IT'S IN THE WORD

Consider it all joy, my brethren, when you encounter various trials, knowing that the testing of your faith produces endurance. And let endurance have its perfect result, so that you may be perfect and complete, lacking in nothing.
James 1:2-4

And not only this, but we also exult in our tribulations, knowing that tribulation brings about perseverance; and perseverance, proven character; and proven character, hope;
Romans 5:3-4

In this you greatly rejoice, even though now for a little while, if necessary, you have been distressed by various trials, so that the proof of your faith, being more precious than gold which is perishable, even though tested by fire, may be found to result in praise and glory and honor at the revelation of Jesus Christ;
1 Peter 1:6-7

For I reckon that the sufferings of this present time are not worthy to be compared with the glory which shall be revealed in us. For the earnest expectation of the creature waiteth for the manifestation of the sons of God.
Romans 8:18-19 KJV

Though he slay me, yet will I trust in him: but I will maintain mine own ways before him.
Job 13:15

Journal/Activity Time

I challenge you to track your progress. Write down where you used to be and your present. Then command your future by writing and saying exactly where you want to be. Remember to always pray!

Day 16
LOVE AND FORGIVE YOUR ENEMIES

Song: **"A Heart the Forgives"** by Kevin LeVar

Quote: What the devil sent to harm you God is going to use to bless you!

Dear Purposed One,

God will fight your battles for you. You should forgive, forget, pray, and move on. I can attest to this because I have been lied to and on. I have been scammed and cheated on. God worked it out in my favor every time. At some point in everyone's life, you will need forgiveness, or you will have to forgive someone. We are all flawed humans walking in fleshly bodies. Because you are not perfect, you *are* capable of making a mistake. God first forgave the entire world for sin (the first sin was committed in the garden of Eden) when He sent His only son Jesus to die on the cross for our sins. A Christian desires to be Christ-like. You cannot be Christ-like if you do not forgive because forgiveness is one of His greatest characteristics. Choose to let go so you can be free and please God at the same time. I realize that there are about six main reasons that we should forgive, and I have listed them below.

1. Forgive so that God can forgive you.
2. Forgive so you can be free. (This is good for your physical and mental health.)
3. Forgive by seeing the need the individual has (empathy).
4. God's punishment is way more effective than anything a human can do, but don't wish bad on anyone. God can help this person grow and get back into alignment with His word.
5. Give grace because we all need it. Also, you probably have done what you're upset about to someone else. We reap what we sow.
6. If Jesus could die for our sin, knowing He had done nothing wrong, we can forgive.

Do not worry about your enemies. God says not to touch His anointed or do His prophets any harm. In His word, He also said He would make your enemies your footstool. As a Christian, you should not wish anything terrible on your enemies; we should pray for them. In my last year of high school, I had a lot of haters and people lying on me. However, they could not stop what God had for me. Many people were saying I didn't deserve this and that, but I knew, and God knew the hard work I put in. The Bible is so true. God will prepare a table for you right in the midst of your enemies. At the honors night, I received countless awards, but the thing that moved me the most was my recommendation letter. It was by a teacher who had died before the ceremony, they presented it at the program, and no one else's recommendation letter was read. In the letter, he talked about how I was such a good student and that he would observe how hard I worked in the classroom. I must also mention that I was the only one to receive this scholarship award. It's like my teacher knew he was going to die because before he did, he dropped off my letter to the counselor's office. When he died, I was so sad and frustrated because I thought I would not be able to get the application in on time, but God already made a way.

I know that it's hard to love your enemies. In high school and college, I held many leadership positions in organizations, and I had to deal with all types of personalities. Out of my frustration, I wrote this in my journal:

The Girl Who Drowned in All Her Success

I am that girl who has everyone's best interest in heart. But no one sees me. I try to be nice and see the good in everyone, but I'm always taken the wrong way. Not only do people misunderstand me, but they are also rude and mean to me. My only desire is for us all to work as a team. I allowed these things to get in my heart and make me angry. I became selfish. It's a dog eat dog world right? At least that's how I felt. Why do I have to do for those who try to take advantage of me? Oh yeah, when I make it forget everybody! No one will understand how hard I've worked to make it this far. You weren't there.

That's no way to live, and that's when the realization came. I asked God to show me myself, and well, I didn't like it! I watched a movie about a girl who was at the bottom. She made it to the top, and she forgot who was there to help her. She turned her back on family and friends, and most of all, God. She finally won, and she felt that everyone was beneath her. She lost herself in this process of becoming successful.

Later on, I felt like Jonathan McReynolds in his 2020 single when he said, "Deliver me from people". He then went on to say, "I don't know the damage or which one to blame". First, I was wrongly accused by people at my job; I prayed and remained calm. Things worked in my favor. Next, I was scammed about two weeks before I left for South Africa, and the items were for my Africa trip. This situation really put me at an inconvenience not only financially, but as far as time too. Once again, I prayed and didn't lose my cool. God worked it out to the point where I received better quality items, and someone else offered to purchase them.

From those points, I prayed, "God, help me love my enemies and hold no bitterness in my heart; let me remember that everything I do is unto You." When you don't forgive, God will not forgive you, and it hinders you from receiving blessings and even deliverance. An enemy can be your footstool and lead you to your next big blessing!

A Short Prayer for today

God,

If anyone who reads this is facing this situation (or ones like this), I pray that they would turn away from it and let You fight their battles.

In Jesus name,
Amen.

IT'S IN THE WORD

You prepare a table before me in the presence of my enemies; You anoint my head with oil; My cup runs over.
Psalm 23:5

The Lord said unto my Lord, "Sit Thou at My right hand, until I make Thine enemies Thy footstool."
Psalm 110:1

When the LORD takes pleasure in anyone's way, he causes their enemies to make peace with them.
Proverbs 16:7

Do not repay evil with evil or insult with insult. On the contrary, repay evil with blessing, because to this you were called so that you may inherit a blessing.

1 Peter 3:9

Journal/Activity Time

I challenge you to tell the devil that you are covered. Remember that you belong to God, and always pray and plead the blood of Jesus. Pray for your enemies or do something nice for him or her and watch how you will be blessed and watch how your heart will change.

Day 17

WHAT ARE YOU FEEDING YOUR SPIRIT?

Song: **"Woke Up This Morning (With My Mind Stayed On Jesus)"** by Mavis Staples

Quote: Keep your amour on, the devil is always busy!

Dear Purposed One,

As a Christian, you cannot entertain any and everything. As God's son or daughter, you are in this world, but you are not of it. Guard your heart against the enemy. I always heard the saying a little leaven leavens the whole lump. That means something can start small and become something so big you can't control it. You must have boundaries and restrictions. What your eyes see and ears hear controls your mind. What enters the mind enters the heart. In the Bible, it says what is in the abundance of the heart flows from it. What is imparted into you is going to come out. The Bible tells us to meditate on things that are pure, lovely, and of good report. How can you produce fruits of the Holy Spirit if you are not living a holy lifestyle?

Your spirit combines two things, which are your mind and heart. What you act out on first enters your mind. I know this to be factual because when I had anxiety, it came from overthinking and negative thoughts. When I focused on the word and promises of God, I didn't panic as much. Think about it like this -- when you want to pass a test, you study. Why? You want to get that information in your mind and act on what you've learned, to pass the test and be successful. What is going in you will be what comes out of you.

The Bible tells us to be holy as God is holy. The enemy is very subtle. For example, if a man is a married man, taking that second look at a woman, not his wife, isn't smart. That second look now opens the door for the enemy to set him up. The Bible says that God has made a way of escape, but we must choose to take it. Something to think about is when you listen to music, and then unexpectedly, you find yourself singing it. I sometimes find myself singing songs I have not heard in years. That is how easy it is for something to enter your heart. In the Bible, a man named Joseph ran out of his clothes to get away from a woman who was trying to make him commit sexual sin. Sometimes you must do what you have to do. That is why the Bible tells you to keep on the full armor because, in the full armor, you are watching what you feed your spirit.

You have to have boundaries and do not compromise with the world. You cannot go along with everything! You have the power to conquer the battle in your mind and produce fruits of the spirit.

Dream: Give The Devil A Black Eye by Feeding Your Baby

In a dream on July 13, 2020, I was breastfeeding a baby that wasn't mine. He didn't want his mother's milk (which was formula milk). He cried and wanted to come back to me. She gave him to me, and I fed him, and he stopped crying. I must mention that the milk was coming out very heavily. I had an overflow of milk. In the dream, I told a friend what happened, and they said something is growing and developing on the inside of you (purpose). I immediately woke up from this dream about to rebuke the devil because I had seen such a strange thing. God told me the vision was from Him. Later that night, God gave me insight and revelation, and He even sent a confirmation through a person.

The Authenticity of the Anointing (Overflow of Natural Milk)

In the Bible, the word milk is significant because we all know of the land of MILK and honey (Exodus 3:17). The promised land represents the abundant life. That is why there was an overflow of milk in my dream. It represents the manifestation of the promises of God because it is the "promised land". My milk was natural and "God made". My milk was pure and authentic. Babies need milk to survive. Babies need the mother to survive. Just as I am a mother in this dream, so are we in the Holy Spirit. We have a nurturing spirit because as Christians we teach, show, and help others grow in faith. Christians do not fit in, and they cannot be like everyone else. When you walk in your real calling, you are more than enough. When God downloads principles into you, you'll be more than enough for you and others.

What is Your baby?

The baby is your soul, purpose, and mind. The devil doesn't like it! The devil doesn't like that you have worth and a purpose, and he wants you to abort your baby or have a miscarriage (Spiritual death).

The Survival and Maturity of the Baby

We are mothers and fathers, and we have to feed our babies. The baby has to receive pure milk. In other words, what we as Christians tell others we have to live. We have to be genuine with our walk-in Christ. We stay genuine by feeding our baby.

How do I feed my baby and give the devil a black eye in the process?

- Increasing your time in worship
- Reading the word often
- Praying often
- Attending church often
- Praising Often

What makes God so good is that he is there with us in trials, voids, hardships, and temptations. Only God can deliver you, and only He can sustain your baby called purpose. You have the food on the inside of you that the baby (world) needs! God specifically showed me that I would feed fresh souls. In other words, newborns in Christ will benefit from my ministry and learn the values that include faith, wisdom, and purpose. God first allows us to taste Him so we can tell others how good His flavor tastes! When you walk in your destiny, you stomp all over the devil's eye! He doesn't want you to feed your baby because he knows if that baby lives to grow into an adult, it will be a force to be reckoned with for Jesus! To God, be all the glory!

IT'S IN THE WORD

Submit yourselves to God. Resist the devil, and he will flee from you.
James 4:7

You are from God, little children, and have overcome them; because greater is He who is in you than he who is in the world.
1 John 4:4

For though we live in the world, we do not wage war as the world does. The weapons we fight with are not the weapons of the world. On the contrary, they have divine power to demolish strongholds. We demolish arguments and every pretension that sets itself up against the knowledge of God, and we take captive every thought to make it obedient to Christ.
2 Corinthians 10:3-5

Be self-controlled and alert. Your enemy the devil prowls around like a roaring lion looking for someone to devour. Resist him, standing firm in the faith.

1 Pet. 5:8-9

"No weapon that is formed against you will prosper; and every tongue that accuses you in judgment you will condemn. This is the heritage of the servants of the Lord, and their vindication is from Me," declares the Lord.

Isaiah 54:17

Put on the full armor of God, so that you can take your stand against the devil's schemes. For our struggle is not against flesh and blood, but against the rulers, against the authorities, against the powers of this dark world and against the spiritual forces of evil in the heavenly realms. Therefore, put on the full armor of God, so that when the day of evil comes, you may be able to stand your ground, and after you have done everything, to stand. Stand firm then, with the belt of truth buckled around your waist, with the breastplate of righteousness in place, and with your feet fitted with the readiness that comes from the gospel of peace. In addition to all this, take up the shield of faith, with which you can extinguish all the flaming arrows of the evil one. Take the helmet of salvation and the sword of the Spirit, which is the word of God.

Ephesians 6:11-17

Journal/Activity Time

I challenge you to fast from anything today that is taking more of your attention than God. Whether it be a phone, TV, person, or game.

Day 18
DON'T LIMIT GOD

Song: **"He's Able"** by Deitrick Haddon & Voices of Unity

Quote: There are many ways you can be effective for the kingdom! Do not settle! Step out of your comfort zone!

Dear Purposed One,

Your faith will push you to your destiny. A limit is a point or level beyond which something does not or may not extend or pass. A limit can also be a terminal point, restriction, and maximum point. Also, a limit can be a value desired or something that is set. For example, when you are driving, you have a speed limit that cannot be passed, or you will get a ticket. Think about this once you spend your paycheck, it's gone. Let me tell you, God is the opposite of a paycheck! You can keep going to Him, and He will never run out. God is not like us! He doesn't have a limit on the highway; He can go as fast as he wants to!

. . .

Let me share a praise break as I reflect over the year 2017. I remember all the goals I set for myself. Seven is the number of completion! I achieved all the seven goals I set for myself in 2017! I looked over or thought about my goals daily. I received salvation as a little girl, but I told God I wanted to grow in my relationship with Him. In 2017, I stepped out of my comfort zone and completed a 21-day Daniel's fast. I was always a leader in the choir, but in 2017 I became a praise and worship leader. It was in 2017 that I decided to spread the word of Jesus with strangers, family, and friends more through a text ministry. I also grew in my faith. I wanted to achieve something honorable and make the lives of others better. I was able to do that by making a significant change in my school through the Student Government Association, which was promoting that first-generation students be able to participate in honor's day events. I was nominated for a prestigious award by the president of my college, and he wrote me a recommendation letter for it. Another one of my goals was to win Homecoming Queen. I took the necessary steps to run, I campaigned, and won! I received a scholarship for my next semester. My other goal was to get a license and car by December of 2017. I took my driver's test for the first time. I'd been driving for a while, but I was nervous about parallel parking. When I took the test, I did it perfectly. It's been a long journey, but I completed it. On top of all that, someone called me to say they were giving me a paid-in-full Toyota Camry as a Christmas gift for maintaining an A average! Jonathan McReynolds wrote a song titled *I'm Not Lucky I'm Loved*. Guess what? I was in the video! I almost wasn't because I sent it in at the last minute, but he told me to send it in anyways! In the song, Jonathan was trying to convey that we should give all the glory to God, which is what I'm doing right now! That is just a small thing for God to do. I am a songwriter, and I just believe that one day Jonathan and I will write a song together. I have not done anything so good. I just decided to serve God with my all. God is not a respecter of a person. If he did it for me, he can do it for you! My God has favored me. I'm just so overwhelmed and in awe. When you delight yourself in the Lord, He will truly give you the desires of your heart! Never limit God; if you believe, it's very possible for you.

On January 2, 2018, God told me not to put Him in a box, and in the year 2019, I have seen why! I started a ministry, went to South Africa, graduated from college, and so much more. God is more than able to move on your behalf! Whether it is a financial issue, school issue, enemy issue, family issue, illness, etc. I know God is able because he did all the things for me! All you need is a mustard seed of faith! Never limit God to one place or thing! We serve a God that can do the maximum and not the minimum! Don't limit God because He can do anything! God blows minds!

I love to dream big because I know I'm not capable of doing what I dream of on my own. When my dreams come true, God will get all the glory. When you have mediocre goals, God does not get any glory out of that because that's what "you're capable of doing". I believe that God will help me to accomplish anything I put my mind to. He's done all these things and then some! I expect and trust God to do way more, and I'm just at the shore right now. God is amazing!

I don't limit God. I always expect him to blow my mind. I serve a big God! I believe that an unprecedented testimony (1 Corinthians 2:9) will come from my life. I dream crazy, and I don't wait for the approval of people. God says move, and I go (Galatians 1:10)!

I expect God to do exceedingly and abundantly above my biggest dream. I just want God to do something in my life that only He can take the credit for it. I'm just a small-town girl out here believing God! I'm like Martin Luther King – I have a dream, and I believe God is able!

If God didn't want you to dream big, He wouldn't have allowed Ephesians 3:20 to be in the Bible. God is a dream filler. You must start somewhere even if it's small. Whatever dream God has given, you go for it! You can have it (Philippians 4:13)! Speak your dreams into existence (Romans 4:17)!

IT'S IN THE WORD

Now unto him that is able to do exceeding abundantly above all that we ask or think, according to the power that worketh in us.
Ephesians 3:20 KJV

But as it is written: "Eye hath not seen, nor ear heard, neither have entered into the heart of man the things which God hath prepared for them that love Him."
1 Corinthians 2:9

Jesus replied, "What is impossible with man is possible with God."

Luke 18:27

～

I can do all things through Christ who strengthens me.

Philippians 4:13

～

Journal/Activity Time

I challenge you to tell at least one person about Jesus and something good he has done for you. Write down some ideas that can improve your school, church, or community, and shoot for them.

Day 19

GOD'S WORKING IT FOR YOUR GOOD

Song: **"Intentional"** by Travis Greene

Quote: God's plans are always better than mine (Repeat this quote)!

Dear Purposed One,

Sometimes God will put you in situations, and you don't see any way it can be working for your good. Sometimes where you don't want to be is where you need to be. I really did not want to go to East Georgia State College. I strongly wished to leave my hometown. I didn't feel like there was anything worth staying for. I soon realized that God had a reason for my being there. I received a full-tuition scholarship to go there. I was there to minister to my professors and students. I had to stay so I could help take care of my grandmother. I would go to her house almost every day during her illness to keep her encouraged, and we would literally have church. She eventually died, and if I would've left, Lord knows I would have regretted not being able to spend time with her. My mother and other grandmother fell very ill, so I was there to support them as well. I just felt overwhelmed dealing with two sick grandmothers and a sick mother at the same time. Thankfully, I was able to stay at my church, mature spiritually, and be a help, and I was successful at East Georgia State College. He placed me at a college with professors who were very understanding when it came to the situation with my mother and grandmothers. I was also able to develop a close relationship with my college president, who was a lawyer and taught law school. My college president aided me in the whole process, and he nominated me for a very prestigious award. God also kept me in Swainsboro so I could become a better driver. I lived a very sheltered life, so God allowed me to gain some more wisdom and experience about how to live life as an adult. God had me there so I could develop overall. I know for a fact that I wasn't ready to go because I wasn't mature enough spiritually. God strategically placed me where I could minister, be successful, spend time with my family, mature me, and make an impact. God showed me that I could make a global impact even though I'm in a small town. God can use whomever He chooses. I didn't see it right away, but it all worked for my good. I was like, "Wow. God really loves me."

IT'S IN THE WORD

For My thoughts are not your thoughts, nor are your ways My ways," says the Lord. For as the heavens are higher than the earth, so are My ways higher than your ways, and My thoughts than your thoughts.
Isaiah 55:8-9 NKJV

And we know that all things work together for good to them that love God, to them who are the called according to his purpose.
Romans 8:28

But as for you, ye thought evil against me; but God meant it unto good, to bring to pass, as it is this day, to save much people alive.
Genesis 50:20

And the Lord turned the captivity of Job, when he prayed for his friends: also, the Lord gave Job twice as much as he had before. Then came there unto him all his brethren, and all his sisters, and all they that had been of his acquaintance before, and did eat bread with him in his house: and they bemoaned him, and comforted him over all the evil that the Lord had brought upon him: every man also gave him a piece of money, and everyone an earring of gold.
Job 42:10-11

Journal/Activity Time

I challenge you to repeat this quote all throughout the day!

Day 20
PURPOSE

Song: **"Try"** by Jonathan McReynolds

Quote: God will not always give you all the details, but move anyhow.

Dear Purposed One,

If you are like me, it is probably driving you crazy if you do not know your purpose. What is life if you don't know your purpose? It is like something in you that makes you feel incomplete or unfilled.

I figured out my purpose through bits and pieces. I knew for a fact that I was created to tell people about Jesus, sing, and write songs, but I knew I was supposed to do more than just that. I began to seek God about my purpose after my grandmother became ill because I felt like maybe she would not die if I got in my right position. So, I began to type articles on what I was feeling and look up scriptures on how to deal with these issues, and I would send them to my family and friends. The messages encouraged them, and to know I was helping someone through my struggles genuinely made me happy. It was then that I realized I was a motivator and encourager.

God placed it on my heart (at the age of 18) to write down my possibilities, gifts, and things that interest me. I wrote down talking, social media, singing, songwriting, and writing. I also wrote down anything to do with fashion, such as hair, nails, clothing, and shoes. I also wrote that people like the way I dress and that people were more attracted to me when I won Homecoming Queen. Under talking, I wrote that I could mentor other young people, motivational speaking, evangelize, preach, and be a lawyer. Under social media, I wrote that I could make posts that encourage people daily to live for Christ. Under singing, I put that perhaps I could travel and sing the songs God has given me. Under the writing section, I wrote a blog, website, and college education. Because of love for writing, why not write a book and start a website to encourage the millennials? Especially since I already send out messages to people daily. As far as college, you must do a lot of writing in your upper levels, so for me, it was just confirmation to me that I will finish college. Plus, I desire to be a lawyer, so that will require me to do a lot of writing. Under fashion, God showed me that the way I carry myself is what will draw people to me like Esther. He has placed it on my heart to start my clothing line one day.

Two years prior, I received a word that I was special and that God likened me unto Esther, but I didn't understand it right then.

Now I understand why God put her in the position to deliver her people. Many people are attracted to me in my generation. Just as Esther was called for such a time as this to help her people, so am I. When they come to me, I tell them about the goodness of Jesus. Just how Esther helped to deliver her people, I am helping my generation. I know that God has more Esther's out here as well.

My passion is helping and encouraging people, and God revealed to me that I was a motivational speaker. God showed me how I could use all these talents and interests to uplift His kingdom. I also realized through the life of Moses and even in my own life that the devil wants to stop a person who has a high call (prince/deliverer) at a young age. He was supposed to be killed (a decree was set in place to kill all newborn male Israelites), but his mother saved his life by putting him in a basket and letting him flow across a stream. He was found by king Pharaoh's daughter and raised him up as a prince of Egypt. I also learned from Moses that we are called to deliver our people. Just as I am called to my generation, you are called to those people around you. In other words, what ever you feel passionate about is what you should concentrate on.

Whatever your purpose may be, know that you can walk in it. You have exactly what it takes. You just have to be willing to sacrifice to succeed. And know this – it's all of our purposes to spread the gospel of Jesus.

IT'S IN THE WORD

Before I formed you in the womb I knew you; Before you were born I sanctified you I ordained you a prophet to the nations.
Jeremiah 1:5

For I know the thoughts that I think toward you, saith the Lord, thoughts of peace, and not of evil, to give you an expected end.
Jeremiah 29:11 KJV

Great are your purposes and mighty are your deeds. Your eyes are open to the ways of all mankind; you reward each person according to their conduct and as their deeds deserve.
Jeremiah 32:19

Many are the plans in a person's heart, but it is the LORD's purpose that prevails.
Proverbs 19:21

And we know that in all things God works for the good of those who love him, who have been called according to his purpose.
Romans 8:28

Journal/Activity Time

I challenge you today to start on the project or vision. Obey God!

A Sneak Peek (Book Two)
A JOURNAL EXCERPT FROM BOOK TWO

Who Have I Become?
11/18/2017 2:07 am

I don't know who I have become, and it hurts so badly. I can't believe he waited three months to tell me why he broke up with me. Soon it will be two years and I'm still not over it. I don't know how to feel. I never knew I could feel this pain. I'm tired of hiding behind this mask. My head hurts, my body hurts. Everyone thinks I'm bipolar because one moment or day I'm happy, then the next moment I'm not. Truth is, in reality, I'm never happy. I'm just faking it, and I don't even have peace to sleep at night. No one knows my pain. My hair is breaking off. All I do is stay in bed in the dark, and I cannot even eat. I'm losing weight. I really loved this guy. I don't even care or feel the need to get cute like I used to.

Life wasn't supposed to be like this. I had pictured the "Perfect Life" in my mind. Life was supposed to be so simple. He was supposed to be in the military, and we were supposed to get married. I was supposed to be his college wife. I cry so much I should be dehydrated. I'm surprised I haven't lost my mind. I try talking to other guys, eating, shopping, and going to church. Why are none of these things working? Is there any solution to this hurt?

*I don't want to be bothered; I just want to be alone. I'm tired of pretending and encouraging others while my heart is broken into pieces. This is so bad for my health. Why me? Why do bad things always happen to me? I feel like I have no purpose to live. I'm just here, and **no one** knows my pain. I'm in college, and I can't even focus. Sometimes I don't even go to class. I've even cried in class, and no one notices. I can't count how many times I cried around so many people, and they don't even notice it. I'm bleeding inside, so I really don't know how much longer I will survive.*

My friend keeps telling me to let it go, leave him alone, and just move on… but I love him. How do you just let it go? This hurts so bad I don't know what to do! I just hate my life! I don't think I will ever love again. Why couldn't his mom just like me? What made me so bad? I wanted nothing more than to love him with my all and support him. This has been the hardest test of my life. I have suicidal thoughts, I've been depressed, my weight has been up and down, I'm tense, I have headaches, and on top of that, my hand hurts, and I'm constantly thinking about it. It's tormenting! And just when I think I'm over him and can talk to a new guy, the new guy screws up or either I just break it off because the connection is not there.

I don't want to lose him, after all, we've been through. Can someone just wake me from this bad dream? The person who reciprocated my efforts and loved me the way I loved him is no longer a part of my life. I'm so tired! I'm so tired! My mom's always like you just need friends, and I'm like no I just want my baby, and I'll be alright. Like there is just no me without him, and it's affected every part of my life.

To be continued…

PART IV

Other

Fighting for My Life: A Test of Faith and Spiritual Warfare
A MORE DETAILED VERSION OF THE SPIRITUAL WARFARE IN UNSPOKEN

I can relate to Deon Kipping as well when he sang, "If my life had a voice and told you my journey you wouldn't believe it and because of His grace there's no way you can see it." I don't look like what I've been through!

In the year of 2018, I went through a mighty trial. My grandmother and mother suffered from gravely illnesses. In March of 2018, my grandmother eventually died four weeks before my college graduation.

After that, I went through depression. I really wanted to go to this school and couldn't go. This was really heartbreaking because I had applied for over 20 scholarships. I felt so hopeless and so unhappy. I felt like life was just too hard! I felt hopeless and got drunk after that. I just wanted the pain to end. I even contemplated suicide. The next week, I wrecked my car, and as a result of this, I lost my job. After that, I experienced a great deal of loneliness and asked God, "why have You isolated me?" He began to show me my purpose, and I began to walk in it.

While walking into my purpose, I lost friends and saw my enemies clearly. I lost sleep many nights. I cried many nights. I felt like I didn't have any support many nights, and somehow, I just kept going. Then on November 18, 2018, the greatest attack on my life began. I had not been eating, exercising, and following a set routine ever since my grandmother died. My body wasn't getting the proper nutrients it needed or functioning properly.

In November of 2018 Right Before the Attack, I Said

I've been really worried about my grades. They had me calling all these different advisers! I'm worried about my grades. I don't know if they are going to accept my three classes!

Grade Situation Resolved

Glory to God! God is so faithful! All my classes were accepted, especially the three I was worried about. I was failing at first, and God helped me to bring up my grades. I had so many reasons to give up, but God! I was so stressed, but God worked it out! God is so Good!

After the Grade Situation was Resolved

On November 18, 2018, a guy persecuted me on YouTube! When I took a stand for God, I also lost a lot of friends in real life and on social media. I lost weight as I wasn't eating. For two months, I was failing my classes, and right before I got sick, they were telling me they weren't going to accept three of my classes.

Meaning, I would have to go an extra semester. Meaning, they lied to me in the first place when they told me they would accept everything. Also, I became frustrated because no one could tell me who my adviser was, and I was just going from person to person trying to get registered for classes.

On November 26, 2018, I assume I became very dehydrated. I was sitting at the table eating with my parents, and I got up because I felt like I was losing my mind. I felt like I was going out of my body, and I began to pace the floor back and forth. It was so scary. I just remember feeling so nervous and tired. I sat back down to eat, and then I went to my bed to go to sleep. It was so scary, and I felt like I was going to die. The next day I started having crying spells, panic attacks, and my heartbeat over 100 beats per minute for 11 days straight. Like if you were beside me, you could literally hear and see my heart moving so fast. I remember thinking I was going to die from a heart attack. I couldn't sleep at night. I would have to get up and walk.

It felt like I wasn't in real life. Like I would literally go outside sometimes to know I was still in real life. That was so tormenting. I suffered from anxiety! I fasted and prayed and fasted and prayed! Nothing happened. Things only got worse. I was having insomnia, nightmares, and crying spells. In my nightmares, I was being chased, seeing my dead grandmother, and my reliving my wreck. I was seeing snakes and other demonic beings. Don't forget, I'm not eating or sleeping, and my body is going up under extreme stress. I had no peace!

. . .

On Christmas day, I isolated myself from my family, and I had never done that before. During this phase, I didn't want to be around anyone. One night I had three panic attacks in my sleep. This was like two days after Christmas, and I said enough is enough. I told my pastor what I had been experiencing, and he prayed for me. The fast heartbeats stopped, but I still suffered from anxiety. I guess it was anxiety. It felt so demonic. I've never been so scared to the point where I'm always anxious like that. The weirdest things were happening to me, such as random sickness, anger, and just petty things related to college. For instance, my computer would freeze in the middle of my test a lot when before I took it, my computer was functioning normally. Also, I had an associate, and that relationship was attacked over the pettiest things. I was so afraid to get up every day never knowing what was going to happen next.

I finally started feeling somewhat of a breakthrough during the first week of January 2019. However, there was still fear, and I was so burned out. Right after this, I had to start my job. Even though I had not fully recovered in my body and my mind, life still has to go on, right? The night before my first day of work, my head was pounding, and I had a nightmare. This affected me greatly because I wasn't as outgoing and assertive as I usually am, but I gave it my best. I completed all my work. I continued to work, school, and ministry.

Just when I didn't think it could get any worse, it did. I started feeling extreme condemnation for old stuff. Like the devil literally flashed everything to me that I ever did wrong in my life. Stuff from when I was really young that I had completely forgotten about. Then after I got over the condemnation, he started filling my mind with evil thoughts and lies. At this point, I was really questioning my sanity. It was like I couldn't stop the intruding thoughts. This went on for months, and no one was able to help me. I was tired and felt so alone and misunderstood. The hurt was so severe I just wanted to die. I was so tired. I kept praying, reminding myself that God would not put more on me than I can bear. I didn't have the strength, and I still wasn't eating, and I was still losing weight. I ended up losing 17 pounds in all. I remember losing hope for deliverance. I remember feeling like God had forsaken me. No one knew how bad I was really feeling. No one knew how bad this 20-year-old wanted to die. I was overwhelmed. I looked to the left, and I looked to the right, and I had no peace.

By this point, I knew I was in need of deliverance. I was helping everyone get delivered, but I couldn't deliver myself. During this process, I had enemies come against me on top of my other issues. They were plotting on me. They even laughed in my face during a meeting when the top boss tried to embarrass me with a lie. At this point, I felt what Mary Mary said in their song, I Need A Little More Jesus, "Problems at work and problems at home. Won't everybody just leave me alone."

Now on top of these other issues, I had to worry about if I'm going to pass my classes. I was also worried about my reputation when I apply for a new job. I felt so much pressure in my head and behind my face through this whole process. I felt like I was going out of my head and face. No one knew I was so tense that I had to use freezer packs almost every day for some relief in my head. On top of that, I also dealt with hypersensitivity. Plus, I would have these weird bodily feelings. It was a heaviness and feeling of so much pressure like something was snatching me. I just had to plead the blood of Jesus and pray daily.

In March 2019 Right Before the Attack Comes to an End

I just remember thinking to myself that this pain will never end. When people would ask me how I was doing I wanted to say, "I'm surviving," but I said, "I'm just fine." My throat began to feel like it was closing up. I just knew I was going to die. I went to the emergency room. They told me I had anxiety, panic attack, and tension. I was so tense, and I know it was by God's grace that spasms didn't start. All they did was give me a Benadryl and told me to get counseling because I was super stressed. The pressure would be so severe that I felt paralyzed. Like, sometimes, I couldn't really feel my eye or jaw. I would even go numb in my hands. I would literally have to use the audio feature on my phone to do homework, work on my book, and whatever else that needed to be typed up. I was determined not to quit!

At this point, I can't lie, I just felt like I was going to a hospital or mental institution. I knew the devil was trying to make me have a nervous breakdown or even a stroke. Don't forget now we are in March the month my grandma died, and I'm still grieving over losing her. Don't forget I'm still praying for and ministering/counseling people. One night, I had to be up at 6 am for work, and a millennial called me saying that they were wanting to commit suicide, and I stayed up with them until about 2 AM. There was another instance when a millennial called me concerning something going on in their life and, once again, I needed to be up at 6 AM to work a ten-hour shift that day. However, I stayed up until 2 AM again. Then on the week, I went to the emergency room, three ladies came to me with problems 3 days in a row. I mean serious issues. Though I was going through a very serious issue myself, I still listened to them and counseled them. God can use selfless people.

Just when I thought it couldn't get any worse, I developed pleurisy in my lungs, which made it difficult to breathe. Like it was so scary because I thought my asthma was coming back! Don't forget I'm still in need of deliverance from the spirit of fear and the other demons that are tormenting me. At this point, I'm scared, and I can't even hear God for myself. Bitterness and frustration started to come in. I was hurt, lonely, misunderstood, and disappointed. I was depressed, anxious, and heavy laden. I don't even know what the root cause was of all this yet. I can only assume that it was spiritual warfare (opposition to stop me from getting to my destiny). During this whole process on January 11, 2019, I asked God why I had to go through all this. Out of the blue, I kid you not, Jekalyn Carr's song, "Greater Is Coming" started playing on my phone. I was not even listening to any music. I was like, "I hear you, God. I'll go through what I have to go through."

I just went under extreme attack. That is all I can say. It was a fight to keep my sanity. God told me an unprecedented testimony was coming from life, prominence, and wealth, but He didn't tell me I would have to go through all this. The devil had been telling me through this whole process to quit Millennial for Christ and to kill myself. Every day I kept questioning my sanity. Every day I just kept saying I wish I could snap out of this. I was in a maze. I was a prisoner. I wanted to throw my hands up and say I quit. I was like, "if it takes all this then I don't want it!" I was at a point like, "devil I'll do what you want just stop tormenting me!" I felt like Kelly Price when she sang the song, I need a healing for my soul. I knew I needed a breakthrough. I even thought to myself why me. God reminded me that it was temporary and that He would get the glory!

On April 2, 2019, God led me to Psalms 88, and that's exactly how I was feeling, but I didn't see a solution. What is the solution? So, I decided to do more research on the author, Heman the Ezrahite. He was wise, anointed, and a man that God used greatly. Heman actually means faithful. I think God was letting me know that He sees my faithfulness.

According to the website gotquestions.org, "the musician and sage Heman served in Israel as a Levite, a seer, and a songwriter. He was a Godly father and a man of influence during the time of David and Solomon. Today, his only known song is Psalm 88, a song of one passionate for God: 'Lord, you are the God who saves me; / day and night I cry out to you' (Psalm 88:1)." Then it clicked in me that God told me I would do all these things. To me, it was God letting me know that He knows me and sees what I'm going through.

God works in mysterious ways. It was deeper than reading the psalm. He was letting me know or giving me confirmation that He has called me. He sees what I'm going through at this very moment. He knows I'm in my lowest pit, but He sees my future. He was letting me know that these are the trials I have to go through for my calling. I didn't see my way out, but God knew I was coming out.

. . .

On April 7, 2019, I wrote:

I am weary. I'm so confused and frustrated. I have given God all I can. I have sacrificed so much. I have changed so much. All I seem to get in return is no breakthrough, tears, warfare, and heartbreak. Things seem to have become worse for me for finally obeying God. I feel abandoned. I feel like I've been left alone to die. I'm tired. I just can't keep going like this. Like do you hear my prayers, God? I'm afraid! I don't understand why so much pain! This weight is heavy! I need to break free! Set me free!

Victory

On May 1, 2019, after *all I had been through* the blessings began to flow. I went to South Africa and raised $6,000 to go. I gained my weight back, made all A averages, and took summer classes for free. I was the first CTAE video success story from Swainsboro High School and the first black female to intern with the DA office and Police department at the same time. My ministry reached 12,000 people, and I graduated early (which was never planned), with honors, and debt-free in December. I must mention on November 25, 2018, I connected with my prominent role model Pastor Marcus Gill. I'm sure the devil did not like it, and to God be all the glory I am honored to have him write the foreword to this book. God is so faithful!

Glory

At 20 years old, I have completed my first photoshoot. I look at my pictures and admire the woman God is molding me into spiritually, academically, and physically! My JROTC Sergeant Robinson always told me, "If it was easy, everybody would do it"! I value this quote he instilled in me in high school. I always

153

remind myself that my success requires hard work and dedication. I'm here to tell you that saying was and is very true! What a journey this has been, but God's grace has been sufficient! From being super involved, remaining honor status, and going to school fully on scholarships has not been easy but totally worth it! I was nominated as a CTAE Success Story, and I was interviewed by the Georgia Department of Education in Atlanta. I am the first to do this from Swainsboro High School because this is something new CTAE is trying. I was also invited to join Phi Gamma Nu. However, I decided not to join due to many other obligations/commitments that I already had at the time. I interned with the District Attorney's Office. Also, I interned with the Police Department, and I was told that I was their first intern. Lastly, not many people knew this, but I was in a serious wreck the year before. God has blessed me with life twice (Miracle Baby)! I'm still doing my ministry online, and God is giving me favor. I don't limit God! This is just the beginning! The devil literally threw everything at me that he possibly could to try and stop me, but he did not succeed! God is doing great things! I am here for a purpose on purpose! He healed my heart, and He healed my mind! He blessed me! He gave me everything He promised me. What a mighty God! Hallelujah!

When It All Falls Apart Seek God and It Will All Make Sense: God is Drawing You to Him Because He Wants to Show You What is in You!

(CORONA/COVID-19 MESSAGE)

2020 is the year of Perfect Vision! Let me be transparent right now! I get what's going on in the world right now! God is simply trying to get the attention of His people. He wants alone one-on-one time with you. Two years ago, God placed me in a position all alone. I lost a grandmother, a material possession that was dear to me, and I even lost friends. I found myself going to school online and isolated. I was stuck in the house, y'all. That was the season that God dealt with me the most. It was in this season God birthed purpose in me. So, no, I'm not going crazy at the thought of being stuck in the house or being isolated. Since I've graduated, I wouldn't go crazy even if I had to do the work online because I've already been there, and I understand exactly what's going on.

What the world is going through is what I experienced in my own life two years ago! God wants you, and He wants you desperately to seek Him! Even recently, I went through a test where I lost something major! God told me He was testing me and get this – I didn't lose as much as I thought I did. Get this though, amid the hurt and lost I was still praising my God! I'll do it all over again because nothing or anyone on this earth is greater than my relationship with God!

2020 *is* the year of Perfect Vision! God is using what's going in the world right now to clear our vision. God teaches you a lesson in everything. The people perish for a lack of knowledge (Hosea 4:6). God wants to give you knowledge in this season so you can prosper! God wants to have a relationship with you (time, love, lifestyle, foundation, repentance, communication, safety, etc.) God wants your heart to be in the right place (get the junk out the trunk, let go of your idols, have more faith, etc.). He also has a purpose for your life! God has a special plan for your life and blessings!

Corona has shown me that in the past few years, I have been on track spiritually. I went through a lot of stuff in the last four years of my life. It's making everything I've been through make sense because I realize God was preparing me. God isolated me, shut down everything in my life, and pushed me to start my online ministry. He allowed everything I went through to get me back in alignment, assignment, and anchored in Him. God is putting people back into alignment, assignment, and anchoring them in him. The things that are transpiring in the world right now is no shock to me. God's allowing the virus to get the attention of people to seek him. I'm doing what I've already been doing – continuing to seek, trust, and obey God!

IT'S IN THE WORD

But seek ye first the kingdom of God, and his righteousness; and
all these things shall be added unto you.
Matthew 6:33

If my people, which are called by my name, shall humble
themselves, and pray, and seek my face, and turn from their
wicked ways; then will I hear from heaven, and will forgive their
sin, and will heal their land.
2 Chronicles 7:14

We Are in the Pre-Tribulation
(NOT THE END OF THE WORLD)

The world is experiencing just what the Bible said will take place. The devil knows his time is short, and we are in pre-tribulation (Matthew 24:9-3, Revelation 12:12). It's only going to get worse. Saints must truly be anchored in Christ. Ultimately, the will of the Father is being done right now, and He is in control. The Bible says wicked people will hold high positions (Ephesians 6:12). Many Christians are upset about Trump being president, but in the word, it states that God puts people in authority (Romans 13:1). I believe God allowed Trump to be in the office to get our attention, to make us more dependent on him. We need Christians to run for legislative offices. Through the chaos, it is the devil's assignment to take Christian's attention off God. Satan cannot do anything God doesn't allow him to. Also, saints should not allow what is going on in politics to worry them. The devil desires to use authority to make saints compromise, but we must fight and stand. Not only does the devil desire to distract us, but he desires to divide us. He knows there's power in unity. Sadly, in law enforcement, there are many evil leaders, and they are taking the lives of many innocent people. The enemy desires for people to become bitter with the government and each other. That takes our focus off God and places it on earthly matters. The Bible says to think on heavenly things that are lovely and of a good report (Philippians 4:8) (Colossians 3:2). Many saints are concerned about rumors of war and hating the president when all these things are mentioned in the Bible (Matthew 24:6). The kingdom's role is to come together, read the Bible, pray and fast for our nation and churches in categories of unity, peace, change, and guidance for leaders.

About the Author

Mikella Hansley is a native of Swainsboro, GA. As a first-generation college student, she earned her Associate's Degree from East Georgia State College, where she was very involved in the Criminal Justice Club, Phi Theta Kappa, and the Student Ambassadors. She worked directly with the city mayor and college president through her role as Vice President and Homecoming Queen of the Student Government Association. Hansley was chosen for the prestigious "All USA" Award by the college president and senators. During her time at EGSC, she was featured in the music video "I'm Not Lucky I'm Loved" by Jonathan McReynolds—her favorite artist.

She graduated early, with honors, and debt-free from Middle Georgia State University in December 2019 with a Bachelor of Science in Criminal Justice. During her attendance at Middle Georgia State University, she had the opportunity to work as the first paid African American female intern for the Police Department and District Attorney in Swainsboro, Georgia. She teaches college and success workshops and she has had the opportunity to share her workshops with prospective students in Johannesburg, South Africa.

Hansley desires to pursue and complete law school for a Juris Doctor. Upon graduating, Hansley wants to establish scholarships to give back to East Georgia State College and Middle Georgia State University. She also wants to create scholarships specifically for African American students. "I plan to create an organization to assist high school students with the undergrad application process. The honor of receiving an education is bigger than me. I want others to be able to afford and have access to the opportunities I had and use them in ways that will benefit their future. I want to encourage people by showing success is achievable even if their circumstances are not favorable. I will be a world changer."

She is a Christian motivational speaker – a Christ representer. Through "Mikella Speaks" and ministry "Millennial for Christ," she has reached over 12,000 people in 24 nations. In June 2020, she was featured in "The Word Network" magazine. Hansley is the first Swainsboro CTAE Video success story and the first from her hometown to speak to an intergenerational group of students and women at KYP and from the Oprah Winfrey Leadership Academy in two cities in South Africa (Soweto and Johannesburg). She is the first African American female to receive an internship with the Congressional Black Caucus Foundation (aka CBCF) from her hometown. She desires to bring more awareness to the underrepresented African American community. She became a member of the National Black Law Students Association (NBLSA) in October 2020.

Celebs/Prominent People

These are the people that have interacted with Mikella or *Millennial for Christ*, whether it has been through affiliation, conversation, liking or commenting on posts, or following her on social media. Her ministry has been noticed by some of these people. She has also had the opportunity to meet them, or be included in one of their projects.

- Marcus Gill
- Jonathan McReynolds (Featured in "I'm Not Lucky I'm Loved" Video)
- Micah Stampley
- Travis Greene
- Brian Courtney Wilson
- Joann Rosario Condrey and Cory Condrey
- Mr. Talkbox
- Bryan Poppin
- HBCU App
- Oprah "Black Women Own The Conversation"
- Students Oprah Winfrey's Leadership Academy
- "Word Network TV Host"
- The Ministry, **Millennial for Christ**, reached 12,000 people
- **MikellaSpeaks** has reached 7,000 people
- *My Life As A Child Of God* blog has reached over 700 people in 24 nations and received over 1,000 views

Mikella Has Been Featured In:

- Forest Blade Newspaper
- Emanuel County Live
- East Georgia State College Website
- Middle Georgia State University Website

Let's Connect!

I'd love to hear from you! Send me an email at
hopeofgodmh@gmail.com.

Website: Coveredbythree.com
Ministry Donations CashApp: $Mikellahansley
PayPal: https://www.paypal.me/MikellaHansley
YouTube: Millennial For Christ
Facebook: Millennial for Christ
Facebook: Mikella Speaks
Instagram: Millennial For Christ
Instagram: Mikella Speaks
Twitter: Mikella Speaks
Facebook: Covered by Three (CB3Series)
Instagram: CoveredbyThree
LinkedIn: Mikellabhansley
Facebook: Singing For God (MikellaSings)
Facebook: Mikella's College Success Workshops
(MikellaEducates)
Instagram: MikellaEducates

Made in the USA
Middletown, DE
06 September 2022

72502133R00119